Quantum Magic

A Guide to Understanding and Practicing Magic

By

J M Conley

ISBN-13: 978-0-9965901-0-5
ISBN-10: 0996590102

We are perched upon the precipice of a new era. Advancements in the study of the human mind progress at an ever quickening pace. Far too many have been quick to discount the tried and true ways of the ancient mystics. Techniques that have been proven time and time again as invaluable. Those who have kept an open mind have begun to unlock the secrets of consciousness and how the human mind interfaces with the external world. Thus, we have Quantum Magic- an ideal paring of cutting-edge scientific principles paired with authentic arcane wisdom. Let these words be your guide as you launch yourself from that precipice into a new era of your own creation.

- Kaedrich Olsen, author of Runes for Transformation

Quantum Magic is a practical and easy to read primer. I've long been curious about ritual magic, but, after consulting several confusing texts, had just about given up on the topic. Conley's presentation demystifies magic and magical practice. His preparatory exercises are marvelous for anyone who wants to improve the functioning and health of their mind and body. What most impressed me, however, was his step-by-step guide in which he walks the reader through every aspect of a magical ritual. I was pleased to find that those books that had me despairing of ever understanding the practice of magic were not on his extensive list of recommended readings. Quantum Magic is most highly recommended.

— Jack Magnus

Quantum Magic is a delightful book for the serious student/practitioner of all things meta-physical. I especially enjoyed the book's thoughtful approach to a subject that goes beyond humanistic understanding. The discussion on objective vs. subjective realities that appears early in the book is probably the most fascinating one I have ever read. Many kudos to Mr. Conley for pulling together all the essential teachings into this single wonderful book!

— Deborah Lloyd

Quantum Magic is an extremely interesting read. It is obvious that JM Conley has studied this subject for years This is more than just a book about magic; it is also about widening and expanding one's horizon and perhaps looking at things in a different way. For this reason, I would recommend Quantum Magic: A Guide to Understanding and Practicing Magic to everyone.

— Gisela Dixon

Table of Contents

To the serious practitioners,

however far along the path they may be.

Acknowledgements

It used to be esoteric knowledge was only passed by word of mouth and so the student always knew his/her teachers by name and vice-versa. However with information now being passed between people via books, metaphysical stores, festivals, the internet, etc., while the student may know his/her teachers, the teacher may never have heard of the student.

Students now have many more opportunities to converse, discuss and interact with others who, although they may not be teachers, act as catalysts to shape or integrate the student's understanding of magic and its practice. Thus, strict pointing to only a few people to acknowledge for one's progress has become difficult.

I thank all the authors I've read over the years that provided me information, views on the metaphysical multi-verse, ways to develop as a magician / wizard and the like. Without them the path would have been far longer and harder to walk.

I thank all the people that I've cussed and discussed with about the whys and wherefores of the working of magic, whether we agreed or not. They have greatly aided me in developing and refining my current understanding. Without them the path would have been less interesting and significantly lonelier.

Last, but not least, I thank my wife. Without her patience, consistent support and, from time to time timely comment, what you now hold would probably never have been written.

Introduction

Why I wrote this book

Having studied the occult for over 50 years, I've always been bothered by the seeming lack of a consistent approach to the doing of magic. As with most practitioners, I've read dozens of books, attended rituals and seminars, talked with sages / crones, and so on, almost always coming away with conflicting views. One says green, another blue. One says waxing moon, another says waning. One says tiger eye, another obsidian. Further complicating things are interactions with gods, goddesses and other entities, the constant enmity between magical folks and 'science', and differences between religious views both within and outside the magical community. I cast about for years trying to find a framework that would make sense of it all.

I found practitioners followed what they had read or been taught by someone, used an intuitive approach that changed from one moment to the next or practices they simply had accreted over time based upon experiences of what seemed to work. This might be called the cauldron approach to magic. But few could explain why they did something, what impact would come from changing it or from adding or leaving something out entirely. That is, there didn't seem to be any coherent theory of magic.

Further, although there has been much information published about the procedures and tools of magical practice, finding information on how to build magical ability is sparse. I felt there should be specific ways to train oneself to become stronger, faster, better at doing magic in the same way one learns other crafts or skills.

To improve one's ability the common thought seemed simply to be: do a lot of ritual, study, and practice (although exactly what was supposed to be practiced was carefully unspecified). This didn't match the view I had from childhood reading about Merlin or Dr. Strange. There was supposed to be some sort of curriculum that, after study, would make one a more powerful magical person, not just give one a bigger catalog of spells. I wanted something that focused on why magic worked and how to become better at the practice of it.

So I began a journey some years ago to try to reconcile the myriad mystical paths, to focus on their commonalities rather than their differences and to understand the foundational concepts that supported them.

What this book is about.

This book presents a coherent and rational system for the learning and practice of magic. It begins by building a framework that explains why magic works the way it does, tying our physical reality to our metaphysical one. Having this structure enables the practitioner to create his or her own spells, customize the ones at hand to his or her specific needs and understand if a spell doesn't work what can be done to fix it. It provides a way to understand what the various pagan paths have at their hearts and it provides a foundation upon which to build one's own path.

This book also explains what capabilities a practitioner must develop to be successful and why these capabilities are necessary for the practice of magic. It offers a complete course for developing those capabilities, integrating and refining them so that the practitioner can tap into and realize the enormous potential of magical power.

Finally, this book shows the practitioner how to access, focus and direct magical energies. It shows the interrelationships between us, the numinous multi-verse and the gods. More, it shows how to use these interrelationships to establish connections, realize goals and to further walk the path to enlightenment.

Who should read this book.

I hope this book will be useful to the novice and the adept alike.

For the novice it provides a way of understanding magic that can easily be customized to any magical path. It doesn't try to force any particular belief or way. It does attempt to give the novice a more direct path to understanding magical practice and better road signs along the way, hopefully saving the novice time, making the journey less stressful and more enjoyable. That is not to say one can be lazy or expect vast rewards from little effort. All paths to true magical ability are hard and not for the faint of heart.

For the adept this book presents a meta-theory for the practice of magic and the development of the magical practitioner. Adepts probably will recognize some concepts and approaches they have seen before or have developed an understanding of on their own. This should be expected for, to be of value, a meta-theory must encompass that which has come before. The power of a meta-theory is it simplifies and generalizes what is already known, makes it more accessible, easier to understand and easier to use. Hopefully the adept will find this book will help refine his or her understanding of magical workings and inter-relationships.

As E.E. 'Doc' Smith might have put it, "For your consideration, I offer you my present visualization of the cosmic all." Within it I hope you will find something of value.

J M Conley,
Colorado, 2015

Magic and the Multi-verse

A perennial discussion within the magical community revolves around how the sciences of physics and cosmology can be reconciled with the metaphysics of magic. This connection is important in several ways, including:

- Most magic is done to affect events in our physical universe. The better we understand how this connection works, the better we can use magic to reach our goals.

- We most easily access and understand the dimensions and frames of reference we physically experience every day. The better we connect our magic to our senses, the easier and stronger performing magic will be.

Thus we begin our journey with the interface where physics and metaphysics meet. The following delves into the science of physics. For those uninterested, please go on to Chapter 2 (Perception vs. Reality).

Contrary to popular opinion, we live in an analog universe not a digital one. Although we have found digitizing information allows us to transport and to manipulate information very quickly and conveniently, in studying magic and the multi-verse the further we move towards a digital approach the further away we get from our true connection with and understanding of them.

The digital approach has created a set of expectations for many that usually aren't appropriate for the study of metaphysics. Three such expectations are:

- Measurability. Science confines itself to the study of those things that can be measured. If something can't be measured, whether due to lack of instruments or lack of data, then to have a scientific opinion of it is probably misleading. Unfortunately what some scientists say is if something can't be measured with current instruments, then it must not exist. They carefully ignore the myriad examples of things that didn't 'exist' until someone came up with a new instrument that could measure them (e.g. the universal background radiation, radio waves, the Doppler Effect). This view is just bad reasoning.

- Repeatability. If something occurs once as the result of a set of actions then it must occur every time that set of actions is performed or it's not real. Magic deals with shifting probabilities. It is, by its very nature, more subtle than a light switch, which is usually either on or off. Magic is more about making a die come up '4' three times in six rolls rather than the mathematically expected once. Additionally, magic is sometimes the result of not only doing a set of actions but also doing them under the right circumstances and at the right time. If all the attributes aren't fulfilled then the magic may fail. Due to this complex and nuanced nature, magic usually doesn't do well in the laboratory.

- Occam's razor. If faced with a set of explanations then the simplest explanation is usually correct. For example, upon hearing of someone making something disappear via magical means some scientists will say it can't be real. They offer the same effect can be done by sleight of hand and misdirection. The faulty reasoning lies in that just because something can be done in one way doesn't mean that it was, in fact, done that way. Sometimes things simply disappear and they aren't hidden in the bottom of the box or in the prestidigitator's pocket. In these cases some scientists, and all skeptics, tend to come up with very convoluted explanations to try to make the event fit their notion of scientific reality, when, correctly applying Occam's razor, the simplest explanation really should be "it was magic".

Is it possible to reconcile the current picture of reality espoused by cosmologists with that of magicians? Perhaps. Perhaps not. However, there are interesting parallels in the two views.

Speaking physically Einstein's $E = MC^2$ states the entire universe is made up of energy. Material, for lack of a better term, is simply slow moving energy. In our universe energy is expressed as vibration. That is, in a wave form:

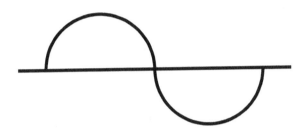

and is the result of the Big Bang, which created the universe and its physical properties.

[sound]

Speaking metaphysically: "In the beginning was the word." The word created vibration, splitting the one into two (an upper and a lower curve), creating at the same time the phenomenon of opposites, leading physically to concepts like inside / outside, fast / slow, strong / weak and metaphysically (duality) to concepts like good / bad, right / wrong, right hand path / left hand path.

The physical fact of energy expressed as vibration has profound implications for the multi-verse, metaphysics and our connection to them. It is a foundational concept that can be used to tie together magical practices and directly relates to that practice, regardless of outward form.

As examples, in a sine wave the area under the top half of the curve must exactly equal the area under the bottom half. Thus, the physical universe is inherently in balance. If this balance is distorted in one space-time then its mirror distortion must occur at some other space-time to bring the universal energy back into balance. We are inextricably connected to the universe because we are made up of its energy. We are also inextricably part of that balance. Thus, karma is not just a metaphysical concept, it's a physical fact. "What goes around comes around" can be illustrated in the wave as:

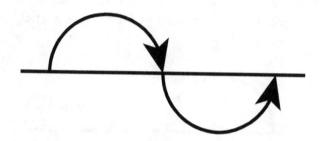

Karma is embedded in the fabric of the universe. Whatever is done that moves the universe out of balance must ultimately come back to restore the balance. However, this balancing isn't necessarily instantaneous or overt from our viewpoint in space-time. Sometimes it is subtle and may occur across several events instead of having a one for one correspondence.

Similarly, many other magical principles can easily be illustrated within the vibrational framework.

Reflection:

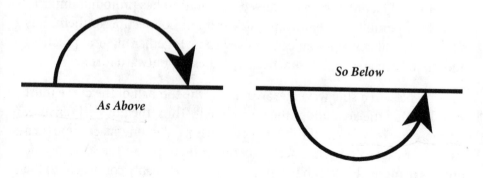

As Above

So Below

Association and Connection:

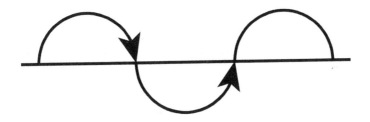

Things Linked Together Affect Each Other

Synthesis:

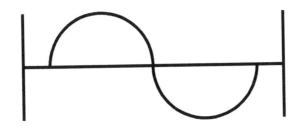

Opposites Unite in the Meta Principle
(Two Halves But Only One Wave)

Unity:

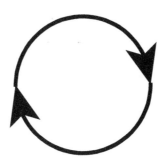

All Things Are Connected.
All Things Are One.

Vibration enables harmony (related vibrations) and resonance (sympa-thetic vibration). As we are vibrations, we necessarily affect and are affect-ed by them. It is through harmonic and sympathetic vibrations that we connect to and affect the metaphysical multi-verse. Changing our energy levels, their frequencies, direction and amplitudes are the foundation of magical work. Many of the differences encountered from practitioner to practitioner are due to how we accomplish those changes.

For example, when our vibrations are sympathetic to another's (reso-nance), we feel an immediate connection, a pleasurable feeling. This shows up in our language. We say things like: "we're on the same wave length" or "we're simpatico".

The opposite usually occurs when we meet someone we instantly want to get away from (dissonance). Usually this dissonance is minor, and we cope with it in a variety of ways. But sometimes certain people's natural vibratory rates are antithetical to others' and can be destructive. Physical-ly, matter and anti-matter instantly annihilate each other, releasing hard radiation. Metaphysically the same can be said of people that are entirely dissonant. As soon as they meet, they tend to destroy each other.

Dissonance can also be used to explain stories about someone suffering ill effect from a demon's touch or withering away when forced to continue contact with a particular person or entity. Resonance and dissonance are real, both physically and magically, and play a major part in the effective-ness of magical practice.

Most magicians have experienced other worlds different from this one. The Kabbalah posits there are 11 worlds. String theory posits there are 11 dimensions. In our dimension we physically access four (length, width, height and time). Each dimension contains an infinite number of uni-verses, each universe having the attributes of its dimension. Conceptual-ly these dimensions and universes are interwoven together, some sitting side by side like the pages in a book. Cosmologists postulate there are ways universes are connected (e.g. wormholes) but nothing has yet been discovered that allows us to use these connections to move between uni-verses.

To understand how dimensions work, let's take a short journey to Flat Land. In Flat Land there are only three dimensions: length, width and time. Mr. Square lives in Flat Land in, appropriately enough, a square house.

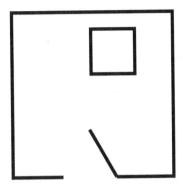

After he comes home from work one evening, Mr. Square closes the door, shutting out all of the trials and tribulations of Flat Land and proceeds to do square-ish things. However, unbeknownst to Mr. Square, you are watching him using the additional dimension of height and can look into his house from above or below, dimensions that Mr. Square cannot physically perceive.

You decide to reach into Mr. Square's house from below. To Mr. Square your fingers would magically appear inside his locked room not just as one entity but five new entities that might look like:

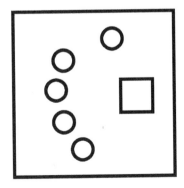

Mr. Square would be totally unaware these five entities were in fact one, as he could not perceive their connection to one another below his plane of existence. When you removed your fingers, for Mr. Square they would simply disappear. Later Mr. Square would not only be unsure of just what he had seen but would probably have a lot of trouble finding the words to explain his experience to his friends. He might say something like:

"I was alone in my room when suddenly five apparitions just appeared in front of me. They were round in shape but not like circle people. They seemed to grow bigger then grow smaller and moved around the room randomly and without purpose. They had similar colors but not exactly the same and their colors changed as they moved. Sometimes they seemed to waver in and out of existence, becoming indistinct. They gave me quite a fright, I tell you, and I couldn't make a sound until after they had disappeared."

Sounds a bit like a ghost story, doesn't it?

Outside mathematics we really don't have ways of describing dimensions beyond our own in plain language. If required to do so we have to fall back on illustration, allegory and metaphor as we simply don't have the words to concretely describe such an experience. Usually such fuzziness is met with derision by those that want clear, concise explanations. After all, why can't you just tell people what happened? Why all the mysterious language?

The tesseract, a four dimensional hypercube, can give us a physical example of this problem. We can illustrate a tesseract on paper (a two dimensional surface) by drawing a line. This shows the first dimension (length). If we draw two parallel lines and then connect them with two more lines 90° to the first two we have added the second dimension (width) and have drawn a square. If we draw a second square above the first and connect all the corners together with lines 90° to each corner we have added the third dimension (height) and have drawn a cube. Note, though, that because we're trying to show a three dimensional figure on a two dimensional surface all the lines are no longer the same length, some are shorter than others and they aren't exactly 90° from each other. To truly show a cube, where all the lines are the same length and exactly 90° to each other, it must be built in three dimensions (e.g. a block of wood). This is our normal reality.

Now a tesseract has a fourth set of lines that connect exactly 90° to each interstice of the cube and are of exactly the same length as each of the lines in the cube. This gets considerably harder to draw. Below is a straight line drawing of a tesseract (a four dimensional cube shown in two dimensions):

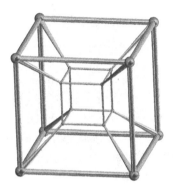

(Figure created using Robert Webb's Stella Software (software3d.com/stella.php)

It has straight lines and looks fairly easy to draw (You might give it a try. It's harder than it looks to get the proportions right.) Note that not only are the lines of different length (the third dimension compromise for the cube) but the outside shapes look more like truncated pyramids than cubes. So although this may be an interesting object it doesn't really describe the four dimensional reality at all well. A closer representation of a tesseract might be:

At least the outer shapes look a bit more like the inner cube. Note how this drawing, although closer to the four dimensional reality, is more difficult to conceptualize and would be considerably harder to describe in words, especially if it were phasing in and out of existence in the other dimensions. We might sound a bit like Mr. Square if we tried to explain it to our friends and only a Physics teacher might readily recognize what we were trying to describe with our words.

As odd as it may sound, cosmologists agree that dimensions above the ones we're used to do exist, even if we can't perceive the extra dimensions directly. Eleven dimensions and infinite universes within each dimension interwoven together, sitting right next to one another; to move between them only requires us to find a bridge.

Magicians tell of visiting other worlds as a common occurrence. Can their stories be reconciled with the dimensional view? For example, what would it be like in a dimension where time didn't exist? Without time there could be no memory and no thought as we know it. You might exist in a sort of stasis, simply existing until some outside force moved you into a place that did have time. You wouldn't recognize your family or friends, remember your life or think about your future. This world seems something like the classical idea of Hades.

What about a place where time was mutable, where an hour in that dimension might be equivalent to a year in ours or an entity native to that universe could make time speed up and slow down? This world seems something like the classical stories of the Elven worlds.

Lastly, what about a place where life force was mutable and an entity native to that place could create / destroy / mutate life at will. Might not we call such a place the home of the gods?

If we can't directly experience a higher dimension's attributes, how do cosmologists know that such things exist? First we can experience the dimension's attributes that coincide with our dimension's four. We can also infer other attributes by observing their effects on the four we can perceive. This approach is how black holes were discovered, by observing their gravitational effect on nearby suns. We may not be able to see them but we can know that something is there and deduce what it must be like by the effects it causes. Experiments using this approach have caused cosmologists to be satisfied more dimensions exist than just the ones we're used to. Experiences by magicians over thousands of years have caused practitioners to be satisfied more worlds exist than just the one we usually live in.

To shift gears, the Kabbalah speaks of 11 worlds. Norse mythology speaks of nine. Most magical models speak of places where physical laws are in some ways different from ours and in some ways the same.

Magicians over the ages may not have approached their magical experiences with the experimental rigor of modern science but to think all of them were superstitious simpletons would, at best, bend credulity. Certainly some of them must have been hard headed realists interested in results and not just mumbo jumbo, especially when one realizes most modern science began with these same individuals. It should be safe to assume some kept good notes of their endeavors (grimoires), full of information painstakingly gathered and validated over repeated experiences. In studying these sources the most interesting thing is that, even though the worlds described are known by different names, the surprising amount of congruence one finds across cultures, time and magical disciplines in the descriptions of these worlds, their attributes and the entities that occupy them.

Cosmologists talk about information theory and how 'information' moves about the physical universe. For example, if a photon of light escapes from a black hole (Hawking Principle) then someone might see that photon of light and information (e.g. existence, direction, speed) would have been transmitted to the observer. Similarly, if a vibration is created in one space-time then that vibration causes resonances both above and below its particular frequency, like ripples in a pond and those ripples can be detected by entities sensitive to the particular wave.

Take a good set of wind chimes and strike only one of them. If they are in tune and you listen closely you'll hear the other chimes begin to sound also. This is an example of resonance. We also have a basic vibratory frequency and can resonate with other events / entities that have frequencies similar to ours. This is the mechanism by which we can become aware of and perceive things indirectly within the multi-verse and other entities can perceive us.

Because each of us has a different basal vibrational rate, this can explain why some people experience certain worlds while others experience different worlds. Our basal rates resonate at different frequencies, so the worlds that naturally resonate with a person's basal rate are the easiest for that person to reach. It also explains why we can reach a particular world only upon the occasion when our vibrational rate is in sync with that of the target world.

To reach these worlds we must add another dimension to our physical four, the fifth dimension of spirit. It is through the spiritual dimension and by using the mechanism of vibration that we gain access to the other dimensions and the universes therein.

To illustrate, let's say we want to establish connection with an entity in a universe that usually operates at a higher vibratory rate than ours. It isn't necessary for us to establish a full connection but only to attract the attention of the entity, by setting up a vibration that creates the proper resonance. This resonance establishes a tone or flare within the perception of the other. Once perceived, the other entity (with a greater vibratory range than ours) can 'tune in' to our vibration, establish a connection with us and drive the communication channel for us. This vibratory connection operates across the multi-verse and transcends conceptual constructs like language. It is something felt from within rather than perceived from without.

Once the connection is made it can be powered by either end or from both ends ("God can't help but hear. He doesn't always listen."). However, a danger lies in that if the other entity is driving the connection, puts too much energy into it, and we have no way to dampen that energy upon receipt, then we can be overloaded and burnt out. This is the mechanism behind stories of people connecting with the gods only to be destroyed by that connection.

Once connected what might we experience? We could easily understand any information that was based in our four dimensions. Things based in other dimensional attributes but close to ours come through almost understood or somewhat garbled. Things based in dimensional attributes outside our experience, and knowledge, come through as noise or gaps in the communication. Our ability to understand is limited by our perception and our 'frames of reference'.

Perception vs. Reality

Is magic real? If it is, how would we know?

To understand the reality of magic question we need two things: operational definitions for 'magic' and 'reality'. Ask most folks what magic is and answers will vary greatly. Ask most folks what reality is and answers may not vary as much but won't necessarily be more useful. Usually the answer will take the form of: "Well you know... it's what's real. Everyone knows what reality is."

Within each of us is an innate understanding of what we perceive reality to be. For each of us that reality is based in our interpretation of our experiences and is 'normal' for us. The key terms are:

- Perception
- Interpretation
- Experiences

We get most of the experiential information we rely on via our senses, but as we age our senses tend to become less sensitive. Gradually our high-end hearing diminishes, our taste buds burn out, our night vision fades. This process is so gradual that most of us don't notice. We cope with these changes, we accommodate and, over time, limit ourselves to them. We forget what it's like to hear the high notes of the violin, taste the complexity of a fresh apple or see the baby rabbit hiding in plain sight. Our ability to perceive changes over time and with it our perceptions also change.

Similarly, what of those that have never been able to perceive the things we have perceived, the blind, the deaf, etc., or have perceived them in very different ways? Their reality must be different, no less rich, no less varied but certainly different.

Most people receive between 75% - 95% of the environmental information they process through sight, with most of the rest gathered through sound. Most of us use our smell and touch senses hardly at all. In contrast, some people have a very sensitive sense of smell and get up to 25% of their information via that sense. How would your reality change if a substantial portion of what you thought of someone was based upon their smell? Would you feel 'blinded' every time you got a head cold?

As newborns our senses are quite limited, the first one we are able to use being touch. Over time other senses (e.g. hearing, sight) become available. As each one becomes available, our brain seeks to utilize the new information perceived to make sense of the world. To interpret what is happening to us and around us. As we have more and more experiences, we abstract patterns from them that allow us to pre-program ways of acting / reacting to our environment. We develop 'frames of reference'.

As we grow, we usually don't compare our senses to those of others. We assume everyone has the same senses we do and that their methods of perception are the same as ours. When someone has the ability to sense auras, to them it's nothing particularly remarkable. It's simply another source of information they incorporate into their view of things. The important thing here is the difference between reality and the mechanisms by which we perceive and interpret that reality. In the above examples reality doesn't change at all; however, differences in what is perceived, how it is perceived and what interpretations can be drawn from those perceptions about reality are significant. Is one interpretation of reality more correct than another? Is one method of perception more correct than another? No, but they do lead people to have very different foci on what is real and how the multi-verse operates.

Each of us has a subjective reality. We must believe in that subjective reality to be able to function, after all it's the only one we have. But isn't there an 'objective' reality? One that's true for everyone? Probably, but we humans aren't very well set up to experience it. We hear a very limited number of wavelengths (roughly 20 – 20,000 cycles per second (cps)). We can distinguish smells numbered only in the tens (a dog can distinguish smells numbered in the hundreds of thousands). We can only see things clearly if they're relatively close to us (i.e. yards / meters) without the use of lenses and can't see them in very fine detail, even up close, without the use of different lenses.

What may be more accurate to say is we have a shared reality we term 'objective'. As with developing our subjective realities, as we acquire the ability to communicate with others we start to compare our views with theirs. We gain confidence in our view the more others tell us they've experienced the same thing in the same way. However we also learn not to compare our reality too closely to the reality of others, for to do so quickly shows that while we agree in general, we don't agree in detail.

(As an experiment get 10 friends together, have everyone look at the sky. Then put each of them in separate rooms with no access to the sky and give each of them a bunch of color swatches so each person can pick out exactly which shade of blue the sky is. After each person selects a color swatch, see if they all match or if there are differences.)

As we do our comparisons we come under increasing pressure from the group to conform to the group's shared reality, even if we don't really see it their way. Additionally we start to find everyone may not use the same mechanisms we do to gather information, and we learn not to talk about any odd approaches we may have (e.g. telepathy, auras), especially if the mechanisms are not commonly available to everyone in our group. To do so risks being branded 'different' and ridiculed / feared / ostracized by the rest of the group. So, we learn to edit the way we perceive things and to limit ourselves to the accepted methods. A good consequence is that our objective reality gets closer to everyone else's over time. A bad consequence is that we throw away perfectly viable ways to experience and interpret our universe in our attempt to fit in. This is one reason children tend to be more attuned to magic than adults.

We find that some of our experiences are quite different from others, especially those found in the alternate realities we encounter. Our society exerts a lot of pressure on us to disregard these alternate realities and only pay attention to the agreed upon 'objective' one. We're told by the group these other places and the events that happen there aren't 'real' and they should be suppressed and ignored. Other older cultures don't do this. Aboriginal Australians actively seek out 'dreamtime'. Amerindian shamans speak of vision quests. Almost all children speak of daydreams.

These experiences may not be as commonly held but that so many of us have them and they occur so frequently shows there may be something of value in them. If our subjective reality is our only truly personal reality, why would we simply throw away any of our experiences? While not necessarily directly applicable to this reality, they might still have value in a variety of ways and probably shouldn't simply be thrown away without consideration. We do need to develop ways of separating what is useful from what is not. We'll come back to this again in a later chapter.

What is an alternate reality? A short answer might be: anywhere that isn't here. Ever sat in your car at a stoplight only to be startled by horns blowing at you because the light has changed to green and you're still sitting there? Where did you go? What were you doing? You weren't here, where were you? The answer is: you were in an alternate reality. Similarly, have you ever had a dream that seemed 'real' (i.e. vivid dreaming)? Could you see, hear and smell things that aren't of this realm but still seemed real to you? This is another example of an alternate reality.

Whereas people used to be far more isolated and information was hidden, modern communication has allowed more of us to realize we are not alone in these experiences. Not only are we not alone in our experiences, sometimes there is an astonishing degree of similarities between experiences by people in very different places and at different times. We are finding others have been to these places and our descriptions of these places, their physical and metaphysical laws and the entities encountered within them match up. We are finding our subjective realities are becoming more 'objective'.

As an operational definition, **objective reality is the intersection between our subjective realities**. It is the culmination of our shared and common experiences. In a very real sense, we create our reality, both individually and in common. This is critical to most magical and religious beliefs.

Most people that have a strong feeling about magic and/or religion can point to one or more events that have occurred in their lives that caused them to believe in magic or in a religion. In the face of skepticism the person almost invariably replies with some variation of, "I was there and I saw it." These are direct and powerful experiences that cannot be gainsaid by anyone who wasn't there and are agreed upon by all that were. They literally are life changing because after them people perceive the universe, and their connection to it, in a very different way. It changes how they make decisions, their values and the way they live in the world. Their subjective reality impacts objective reality with every interaction and becomes part of the objective reality. As an operational definition, **magic is making one's subjective reality an integral part of the objective (group) reality**.

Obviously solitary ritual can lead to powerful subjective experiences. More important though is correctly conducted group ritual also creates a powerful experience for all who participate. After ritual, participant accounts are remarkably similar as to what was experienced both physically AND metaphysically. People agree on what happened, and they share the experience. When they leave the experience becomes as much a part of their view as going to work the next morning. After all, "they were there and they saw it". Thus, if for no other reason, magic is real for the simple reason that its impacts are real.

Perhaps the best known example of how subjective reality became integral to our objective reality began with a carpenter. There is no historical record of this carpenter, so we don't know if he existed in our objective reality, nor was most of his story written down by those that, supposedly, had any direct contact with him. Almost all of what we know of him and his 'miracles' has come down to us through many layers of editing, revising and augmenting.

But, over time, many, many people have had subjective experiences that match up with those stories and have experienced things that cannot be explained by science. They have told others of these experiences and how they were there and they saw it. Others have come to believe these stories with so much force that now roughly 1¼ Billion people say they believe in this carpenter that 'objectively' may not have even existed some 2,000 years ago. **Magic.**

Developing Esoteric Abilities

The practice of magic is an expression of the practitioner. It is both a science and an art. The science is in the approaches, tools and rituals that have been developed over the ages. The art is in the customization of that science needed for the practitioner to succeed. As each of us is unique, our specific magic is also unique. Magical ritual done by a group does not change this. Group ritual is a blending and interweaving of individual threads to make a tapestry of magical will.

To become an adept, you must learn the science of magic. There are numerous books, etc., already existent that delve into this area of study. You must also develop experience in magical work to know what customizations work for you, along with how and when those customizations must be applied to achieve results. Although not as numerous, several books exist that, at least, touch upon this area. Last, you must also develop esoteric abilities to be able to actualize magic in the multi-verse. There seem to be very few sources of information on this area. Yet, developing your esoteric abilities is the most fundamental and important task in becoming an adept. Without these abilities your magic will probably be weak and ineffectual. Esoteric abilities enable you to be more powerful in the mundane world as well, and so are good to develop in any case. They help you become a better person and a better magician.

Adepts will tell you that to perform magic requires the ability to visualize. Perhaps more correct would be to say you need to be able to 'sensorialize'. That is the ability to engage all of your senses to connect to, relate to and understand alternative realities. Several mental abilities are required to do this, including:

- Awareness
- Memory
- Focus / Concentration
- Visualization

The development of other abilities is embedded in building these four. These four will be the focus for this primer. The novice should work on these abilities daily and seek to understand how each adds to the others in doing magical work. Once a basic understanding is in place, the novice and adept should work to improve his/her ability by increasing his/her:

- Sensitivity
- Clarity
- Range
- Power
- Focus
- Capacity
- Speed

Actors are taught the concept of 'sense memory' and spend many hours practicing calling up and reliving sense memories. This helps get them in touch not only with their senses and their emotions but with reality also.

Take the simple task of pumping water into a bucket, carrying the bucket across a yard and pouring the water into a barrel. Try to act out this sequence while staying fully engaged in the sense of it. Try to make it so real an observer would not only know instantly what you are doing but would be so taken in by your 'acting' they would enter into the reality with you.

Did you place the bucket on the ground or hold it while filling it up? If you held it, did you feel the weight of the bucket change as it filled? Did you feel the humidity in the air change due to the water being exposed to the air? When you walked, did you lean to one side because of the unbalancing effect of the weight? Was your head leaning the other way? Did you switch hands halfway across? When emptying the bucket, how far apart were your hands so you could grasp the top and the bottom to tilt the bucket? Did they stay the same distance apart throughout or did you forget you were holding something rigid? Did your stance and arms change as the bucket got lighter? Did you get some of the water on your legs as it emptied? Did you think about how you now had to go get another bucket… and then another… or were you glad you had completed the task and think about where you were going to leave the bucket? All of these things are integral to the task and, whether we realize it or not, engage our senses when getting a bucket of water.

The next chapters offer explanations and exercises to help build your mental, physical and psychic abilities.

Through developing awareness, you will be far more able to connect to physical and metaphysical worlds and to tune into the subtle vibrations that make up magical nature.

Through developing memory, you will be far more able to keep and access the fruits of your increased awareness (as well as remember where you left your car keys).

As has been said, in most complex matters "the devil is in the details". Superior awareness and memory, along with focus / concentration, help make sure the details are covered. Most powerful magic requires intense focus to harness, manifest, direct and release magical energy. Sometimes this focus must also be maintained for a significant amount of time. Through developing the ability to focus / concentrate, you will be far more able to control esoteric connections, manifest magical energy and accomplish magical goals.

Awareness, memory and focus / concentration all come together to generate and maintain visualization. The more sensorially complete a visualization, the more vibrant and detailed it is, the more 'real' it is. As with all metaphysical endeavors, the efficacy of magic is driven by one's belief in it. The more real it is to you subjectively, the more real it will become objectively.

The following chapters on developing awareness, memory, focus / concentration and visualization help you build the critical abilities necessary to accomplish the magical rituals mentioned further along. For those readers uninterested in these areas, please feel free to skip to Chapter 8 (Magical vs. Psychic Abilities).

Before constructing our house of esoteric abilities, we must create the foundation. The first ability is stillness. Magic flows from stillness. It is only after one becomes still one can sense and synchronize to the subtle vibrations, harmonies and resonances necessary to perform strong magic. Even once one has learned how to become still, maintaining this inner stillness is difficult in the face of all the distractions normally faced on a day-to-day basis. That is why all major pathways have some aspect that aims at creating stillness, usually either through meditation or through prayer.

To start the process the novice should find a place and time that limits distractions as much as possible. The objective of this practice is to simply clear the mind, to become 'in the moment' and to achieve stillness. Several approaches are enumerated below. The list isn't exhaustive. If you have another approach that works for you, by all means use it instead. It isn't necessary to do all of them but it is good to experiment so you'll know how you react to each one. Probably you'll find one or two work best for you. Begin with short practice sessions (10 minutes) and progress to longer ones as necessary until you achieve success. Once you have the knack of it you should be able to achieve stillness in a moment or two. For most people it is getting the knack that is hard to do.

 Practice One

Wear comfortable clothes that don't bind you. Go to your practice place and assume a comfortable position (but not so comfortable that you fall asleep).

If seated, don't slump. Imagine you have a cup of water in the middle of your pelvic girdle. Position yourself so you won't spill water from the cup. Your spine should have a nice S curve to it (unless you have some sort of medical condition). Your shoulders should be level. Your head erect with your eyes looking slightly downward. If seated on the ground some people prefer to have a small, firm pillow under them. By sitting a bit forward on the pillow and dropping your legs off the forward edge, you should find it a bit easier to get your pelvis positioned properly.

If lying, your arms should be at your sides. Some people prefer to have their palms pointed towards their bodies. Others prefer the palms point upward. Do whichever feels most comfortable to you. Similarly, some prefer to put a small roll of cloth (wash cloth, hand towel) under their neck to cause a small upward tilt to their head relaxing the neck muscles and opening the airway a bit.

There are a multitude of esoteric positions, mostly from Yoga, that you may attempt. If you find one of these more comfortable, feel free to use it. However, simply sitting or lying down will work fine for this practice. Next,

RELAX !!!

Feel how you probably tightened up upon reading that. You can't order yourself to relax. You have to let go. One way to let go is to take an inventory of your physical body. This inventory is also a good way to become aware of your body and to develop better control of it.

Start with your toes. There are muscles attached to ligaments and tendons attached to each joint in your body. Muscles can only contract. So, usually there are two sets of muscles (agonist and antagonist) for each joint. When the joint goes one way, one set of muscles contracts and the other relaxes. When the joint goes the other way, the reverse happens.

Move your toes back and forth. Feel which muscles tighten in your foot and calf with each motion. Find the position where both sets of muscles are in balance, with the least tension being exerted by each side. This is what 'relaxed' means. It doesn't mean the absence of tension, but the balancing of it. (Otherwise when you relax while standing you'd simply fall down.) Capture and hold onto this feeling. To relax you first must have a visceral understanding of what it means, what it feels like.

Next, concentrate on the muscles in your foot. Flex your foot. Try to touch your big toe to your smallest toe. Try to touch your toes to your heel and then to your shin. Feel which muscles tighten in your foot and your calf with each motion. Find the position where those muscles are in balance with their counterparts, the place where the least tension is exerted by each side. Capture and hold onto that feeling.

Next, focus on your ankle. Joint by joint, muscle by muscle find and capture the feeling of what it means to be relaxed. Don't forget your nose and your eyelids. Make sure to wiggle your ears and your eyebrows. Work EVERY set of muscles. Being relaxed isn't a matter of having no tension but one of having balanced tension. This state of relaxed awareness helps the mind to move into its Alpha state, the state suitable for light meditation.

Having relaxed the body, you can now move on to relaxing / calming the mind. The frenetic pace of modern life has become so ingrained in most of us we no longer think of it as being unusual even if we're aware of it at all. Some of us are continually on the edge of 'information overload' where everything simply blends together to become white (i.e. background) noise. The task is to take that raging river of thoughts and sensings and change it into a calm pool without even a ripple marring its surface. A far more difficult task for most than it might seem.

The first step is to become aware of the thought process. Thoughts, impressions, sensings seem to pop up everywhere in our minds. Imagine them flowing across the screen of your mind. Some move quickly, some slowly. Some are big, others small. Some are clear while others are fuzzy. Don't try to stop them. Let them come but don't hold onto any of them. Let them go. No matter how important they seem, let them go (unless it's the building is on fire or some such). You can deal with them later. Right now let the white water of the river of your thoughts become wider, slower until it settles down into a pool. Let the ripples on the surface of that pool flow outward until the center becomes calm. Let the calmness of the center flow outward until the entire pool is calm. Experience the pool of reflecting water. Imagine the moon being reflected by the surface of the pool. Perfectly reflected, every detail clear and sharp but the pool doesn't try to hold onto the moon. It simply accepts the moon's image and without attempting to change it, reflects it back.

Practice Two

As above, comfortable clothes, comfortable position, practice room and relaxed physical body. In this practice, you'll use an auditory focus to help calm your mind. Three commonly used foci are: breathing in a rhythm; engaging in chanting; or sounding a mantra (e.g. OM (AUM)). However, any repetitive, easy sounding will probably work. Start with 5 minute sessions and increase as you get more attuned to the effects of the practice.

There are many esoteric breathing patterns taught as part of meditation practice (mostly through Yoga and Zen). We will use a straight forward 2 count cycle (inhale for 2 beats, hold for 2 beats, exhale for 2 beats, hold for 2 beats). Breathe deeply and slowly. Stay with the count. If you start to feel tingling or lightheadedness, you're beginning to hyper-ventilate (i.e. have too much oxygen in your blood). Slow the beat down and/or increase the hold cycles to allow your body a bit longer to process each breath.

Each of your lungs has an upper and lower chamber. Focus on cycling the air into the lower chambers. When doing this pattern properly, you should see your abdomen rise (inhale) and fall (exhale) rather than your chest. The purpose of breathing is to allow oxygen to flow into your blood stream and carbon dioxide to flow out. In the hold portions of the cycle, visualize this chemical interchange occurring.

- Inhale: through your nose. Feel your diaphragm pulling your lungs downward, creating a vacuum for air to rush into. Feel the life-giving oxygen entering your body, filling your lungs. See the fresh oxygen passing through the membrane wall of your lungs and into your arteries making the blood red.
- Hold: feel the oxygen being pumped through your body with your arterial blood flow. Feel the oxygen being taken up by your muscles and organs. As the oxygen enters, feel the carbon dioxide leaving, completing the exchange. See the blood change from red to blue and enter the venous system. Feel the blood pass by your lungs and the carbon dioxide migrate through the membrane to be expelled upon exhalation.

- Exhale: through your mouth. Relax the diaphragm, allowing your lungs to deflate and collapse. Tighten the abdominal muscles forcing the air out.
- Hold: processing oxygen takes time. Give your body 2 beats to use the oxygen just received.
- Inhale: relax your abdominals and tighten the diaphragm pulling your lungs downward…

Focus on maintaining the breathing cycle. Once the rhythm has been established, you should be able to maintain it without actually counting. However, to begin with, ensure each part of the cycle is of equal length. As the rhythm takes over you should also feel your mind calming and distractions fading away. If you find distractions don't fade or return, add the approach used in Practice One above.

(As a side note, when we sleep we tend to breathe more shallowly. Doing 3 or 4 cycles of this breathing pattern upon waking will clear your lungs of residual carbon dioxide and invigorate your body and mind by giving them a shot of oxygen, getting them fired up for the day.)

Using Chants:

If you follow a path that utilizes chanting, the hold portions of the cycle disappear, and the chant is added to the exhale part of the cycle. Thus, the cycle becomes inhale and chant on the exhale. Unlike some singing, the inhale shouldn't be a quick forced breath but a relaxed inhale. The chant drives the exhale with the lungs being empty at the end of the chant cycle. Again, focus on the chant. Fairly quickly conscious effort to do the chant shouldn't be needed. As the chant takes over you should also feel your mind calming and distractions fading away.

(As a side note, some people substitute using recorded music for the chant. If this works for you, please feel free to use it. However, I tend to dislike it because it requires relatively sophisticated external equipment and electricity (the ever present 60 cycle hum) that, at least for me, tends to get in the way of achieving true stillness.)

A mantra can be like a chant or simply be a single word. The mantra 'OM' (pronounced AUM (ahhhhooooommmmm)) is well known and illustrates an important aspect of vocalizations. In performing this focus, one should be in a seated posture with the body relaxed.

- Inhale as described above.
- Relax your jaw muscles allowing your mouth to open fully.
- Without strain, tone the syllable "AHHHH" until roughly ¼ of your breath is used up.
- Without strain, allow your jaw to close halfway and your lips to extend into making a strong "OOOO" sound. Maintain this sound until roughly ¼ of your breath is used up.
- Without strain, allow your jaw to fully close (your upper and lower teeth should be in contact) with your lips resting together. Allow the "OOOO" sound to naturally change to "MMMM". When done correctly (teeth together) you should feel the sound resonate throughout your skull as if something was vibrating in your head.

This powerful technique helps relax the entire body and causes the mind to generate Theta (deep meditative) waves. In times of stress, do this technique 3 or 4 times to help re-center. Additionally remember the tone you use for the 'AHHH' step. This will probably be very close to your natural basal vibratory rate (more on this in a later chapter). Once attuned to this approach, you may find your ability to attain stillness only takes a few cycles to achieve.

 *Practice Three*

Some people find a visual focus works better for them than an auditory one. Common visual foci include candles and intricate drawings (yantra). An example of a sri-yantra is:

To achieve stillness, place the visual focus slightly below eye level, far enough away so your breath won't disturb it but close enough so it fills as much of your field of vision as possible. This helps cut down on any visual distractions there may be. Lighting should be dim enough so there is no harshness or glare while allowing the focus to be seen easily. Unless using an esoteric standing pose, most find being seated the easiest way to do this type of practice.

Although a breathing cycle isn't strictly necessary for this method, the cycle used in Practice Two may help.

- Seated comfortably in your practice room, settle into an easy slow breathing rhythm.
- Allow your attention to be drawn to the focus. Allow the focus to become the center of your attention, filling it up to the exclusion of all else.
- Allow yourself to enter the focus so that instead of being in front of you it becomes all around you, shutting out all external distractions. You and the focus are all that exist.
- Inside the focus all is stillness. All is calm. Feel the stillness become part of you until you are one with it.

Practice Four

For this practice you will need a chime or tubular bell, the longer, heavier (lower note) usually the better. You want a chime that will sound for a reasonably long time. Sounding duration is a function of the size and quality of the chime. You will also need a way of striking the chime. A felt covered drum stick (the kind used for striking a kettle drum) works well for this purpose. Hang the chime in front of your sitting place within easy reach. Sit comfortably and settle into an easy, slow breathing cycle.

- Close your eyes and sound the chime.
- Focus on the tone of the chime. Feel its vibration. Allow it to wash over you. Attune your vibration to it so that you become one with it. The closer the chime tone is to your natural basal tone (see AUM above) the easier this should be to do.
- Gradually the tone will grow softer and softer, stay with it. Visualize the ripples of sound expanding outward into the universe, leaving stillness in their wake.
- Eventually the chime will fall silent. Stay in the space between the sound and the silence. Stay in the stillness. Become one with it.

Once comfortable with this approach you may find it to be the easiest way to get into a deeply meditative state, requiring only one or two soundings to accomplish the change from the Beta (awake state) to the Theta (deep meditation) state.

Awareness

Having learned to achieve stillness, the next step on the path is to develop awareness. Being aware is using all of your senses to connect with and gather information about your environment. The better you are at doing this, the richer your perception and appreciation of, and the more complete your connection to, the universe can become.

Strangely we tend to disconnect ourselves from the universe rather than connect. Because we have consciousness, we perceive ourselves to be separate from the universe. More, we establish several divisions between the universe and ourselves. We say "I am in here" and the universe is out there. Then we say: "I am divided into my body, my mind and my spirit." Further we say: "my mind is divided into my super consciousness, my consciousness and my sub consciousness." Lastly we say: "my consciousness is divided into waking consciousness and the 'observer' that watches what I do in my waking consciousness." Is it any wonder with so many divisions we feel disconnected?

But these artificial divisions, these abstractions, are not real. They are merely constructs we put on ourselves and that lead us away from the path. We are like a wave in the ocean that focuses on the impression it is smaller than other waves, slower, unlikely to go as far, all the time forgetting it is an integral part of the ocean and, thus, a part of all the waves and the entire ocean.

Physically you cannot show where you end and where the universe begins. There is a constant interchange between the atoms that make up your body and the atoms that make up the world. Your cells consistently and constantly migrate out of your body in such a way that each and every cell in your body is replaced approximately every seven years. Every seven years physically you are a completely different person.

You come from the universe, are always an integral part of it and ultimately return to it. Your mind and spirit resonate with the music of the stars as it impacts you and you, in turn, impact it. Thus, you do not have to 'connect' to the universe or its magical power. In a very real physical, as well as metaphysical, sense you are one with the universe, and so are always connected to it. To be disconnected means that you would no longer be part of this universe. We are, as Carl Sagan put it, "made of star stuff." What is necessary is to become aware of that connection, become sensitive to it and how to use it to accomplish your goals.

In school we learned there were five senses: Sight, Sound, Smell, Taste and Touch and, thus, assumed that was all we could use to interface with our world. Actually there are several more senses we use every day. For example we have senses of balance, direction and time that we should also develop.

Human potential is vastly underrated by most. Our abilities, when used to their fullest, are astonishing, but most of us only use a fraction of them. As examples, in pitch blackness our eyes are capable of seeing the light of a match at a distance of nearly a million miles and, given appropriate time to adjust, our eyes can respond to a tremendous range of light intensities (a ratio of roughly ten trillion to one from most intense to dimmest).

By touch we can tell the difference between two surfaces that are only .0001 inch (one ten thousandth of an inch) different in height.

Physically, we are capable of running over 15 miles per hour and can sustain a bit slower pace (10 miles per hour) hour after hour after hour (imagine being able to run 150 miles or more in a day). We can lift between three and four times our own weight and jump almost 25 feet.

We have similar mental potentials. We store in our memories EVERY experience we have ever had. We can read 50,000 words a minute (i.e. we can read the average popular fiction novel in roughly 2 minutes) at above 95% comprehension. We do incredibly complex calculations with lightning speed and, perhaps most important, learn new things at an amazing rate.

And yet most of us never use a fraction of our potentials because, in many cases, we don't believe we can, and so we set our expectations far too low.

In the early 1960's an experiment was done as part of people studying foreign languages to see how many new words could be learned in a set period of time using advanced learning techniques. A base line of 60 – 75 new words per day was established with an expected 87% retention rate. By 1977 test subjects were learning 3,000 words per day or roughly 375 words per hour. Most study courses assume the student can only learn 20 – 30 new words a day. (As a side note: the average high school graduate has a vocabulary of around 2,000 words.) Obviously the bar is set too low. Our task is to set more realistic expectations and then achieve them.

To be able to more powerfully interface with and connect to reality, we first must become aware of it.

 Practice One

For most people the vast majority of their sense input is visual, so much so that the other senses are mostly ignored. For this practice, when at home simply close your eyes and pretend you're blind for a while. Try to go through all of your normal activities without using sight. Immediately several things will become apparent, among them:

- How important it is to keep clutter out of traffic patterns.
- How important it is to keep things where they belong so they can be easily found.
- How some activities must be looked at from a very different perspective (pun intended). Things can be done, but how they are done changes. For example, by folding paper money in different ways (e.g. lengthwise, in half) you can tell the difference in denomination without being able to see the bill. Similarly, when pouring a cup of hot tea or coffee, place your

thumb on the lip of the cup. As you pour (slowly until you get the knack of it) you'll be able to feel the heat of the liquid as it gets close to the top and use this as a signal to stop pouring. You have the advantage that, in the beginning, you can cheat a bit and open your eyes to check visually how well you're doing.

Explore this practice thoroughly; after all, the blind handle their lives this way all the time. It can be done. You'll probably find your senses of touch, hearing and smell will become more important and your memory will be required more. You should fairly quickly develop a mental map (visualization) of your home that allows you to move about almost as easily with your eyes closed as with them open (a handy skill to have when the electricity goes out).

 Practice Two

We normally look at things in either a general, big picture way or in a focused, detailed way. When focusing (e.g. reading this book) we deliberately exclude everything else. This can be done with hearing also. We sometimes do this when at a gathering when we start a conversation with someone and then the noise level in the room increases. Even though many people are talking loudly, we can still understand what's being said by the person we're talking to on the other side of the table.

- Listen to the sound of the wind in the trees while ignoring the sound of cars passing by.
- Listen to the sound of your heart beating while ignoring the sound of the television.
- Listen to the conversation at the next table in a restaurant while ignoring all the noise around you. (A particularly useful skill for spies and gossips.)

After you have learned to focus your hearing, combine this with stillness to hear your world better.

- Can you hear your cat's breathing as it lies upon your lap?
- Can you hear the footfalls of your friend when you take a walk together?
- Can you hear the bubbles of your soup while it's cooking?

Sage: "Can you hear the grasshopper at your feet?"
Novice: "Old man, how can you hear such a thing?"
Sage: "Young man, how is it that you do not?"

 Practice Three

Most of what we call taste is, in fact, a function of smell, so both senses will be explored in this practice. As with sight, modern life overwhelms us with smells, most of which are not pleasant so we learn to turn off our sense of smell. We have come to think that most strong smells are 'bad' smells. People who have grown up on farms don't really understand why city dwellers have no tolerance for the odors of nature. Yet, some of our most vivid memories can be triggered by smells (e.g. fresh bread baking, the smell of the air just before and after a rain, fresh mown hay).

Dogs use smell as their primary sense to make sense of the world. Dogs can distinguish between hundreds of thousands of different smells, remembering individual smells for years. As any dog will tell you, your nose works better if it's a little wet. When you lose a scent, wet the end of your nose slightly and take another sniff.

- In spring go to a flower garden. Stand in the middle and smell the garden. Follow the strongest scent you find back to its source. Connect the scent with the corresponding visual impression in your mind. Later, close your eyes and see the flower in your mind, can you smell its fragrance?
- Before eating take time to smell your food. Wine connoisseurs take time to establish the bouquet of the wine and talk about the wine's 'nose'. This exercise has two other effects: it

will tend to slow down your eating pace a bit and, hopefully, make eating a bit more enjoyable; secondly, if taking time to smell your food doesn't put you off fast food nothing will.

- Each time you go to an herb / incense / perfume shop, take time to smell a few of the products (only a few at a time, as your sense of smell is fairly easy to overwhelm, especially with strong odors). Fragrances like sandalwood or lavender are easy to distinguish, but how about other smells (e.g. parsley, sage, rosemary and thyme). Connect smells with tastes with visuals so with any one sense you can call up the others.

 Practice Four

In modern life we normally use our sight to identify objects. That is, we see something, compare it to our abstractions of reality and conclude "that's a tree," "there's a car coming towards me," or "that's the store I'm looking for." We rarely simply allow our sight's information to flow without looking through the artificial overlay of abstraction.

- Go outside and sit in a comfortable place with as few distractions as possible. Close your eyes. Move your head / body so that when you open your eyes you won't be looking at the same scene as when you closed them. Open your eyes and focus on seeing only colors. How many shades of green do you see? White? Blue? How do the colors merge / change from one to another (i.e. are there sharp demarcations or do they blend through a series of pastels)?
- Sit in your living room in a comfortable position when there are as few distractions as possible. Close your eyes. Move your head / body so that when you open your eyes you won't be looking at the same scene as when you closed them. Open your eyes and focus on seeing only shapes. How many shapes do you see (e.g. circles, triangles, squares)? How many shapes do you see within shapes (e.g. a TV might be a square inside a rectangle (cabinet))?

- Get a stool to stand on. Lie on your stomach on the floor and look around you. See the room as a baby would see it. Next, sit in a chair and look around. See the room as a child would see it. Notice how your perspective changes. Some things that were hidden before come into view. Some things disappear from view becoming hidden. Next, stand up and look around you. Last, stand on a stool and look around you. How would your impression of the world change if you only had one of these views and could never experience the other ones? How would your approach to interacting with the world change?

 Practice Five

We all know of the mind / body connection. However, in the West, many times there is an unstated assumption that the mind conceives of something and then kind of forces the body to come along. The idea one can first learn something physically that, then, teaches / changes the mind isn't so well used. Many eastern endeavors (e.g. yoga, martial arts, Zen) are based in the latter approach. Physical experience informs metaphysical knowledge. For the purposes of awareness, we will look at a few simple beginnings.

- Most people don't have a good understanding of how big they are, how far they can reach, etc. To help build spatial awareness stand a few steps away from a wall, with your arms at your sides close your eyes and walk towards the wall until you feel you could just touch the wall with your outstretched fingertips. Stop, open your eyes and try to touch the wall to see how well you did. Most folks find it takes a few tries to get this one down. When this one becomes easy, try doing the exercise while starting from a sideways or backwards position. Harkening back to Practice One, when facing forward, add a sharp, short whistle before each step. Can you hear a difference in the echo as the sound rebounds from the wall?

(Bats use this type of sonar all the time. Shouldn't we be able to also?) Can you use this to help tell how far away objects are? Next, try to do the same exercises but use your foot to touch the wall rather than your hand.

- Stand on a level surface. Extend your arms outwards to the sides. Stand on one foot. When you find your balance, slowly move your arms forward or backward. How does your balance change? Returning your arms to the original position, lower them to your sides. How does your balance change? With your arms at your side, look up, down and around using only your eyes. (If you tend to lose your balance, it shows how much your reliance on your sight affects your world.) Next, look up, down and around by moving your entire head. Stand on the other foot and repeat. Last, try the above while extending the raised foot and moving it to the front, to the side, and then to the rear.

These body exercises are not supposed to start you on the path of becoming a world class athlete. They are to highlight how much we generally ignore the kinesthetic aspects of our reality, even though our kinesthetic abilities enable much of our physical interaction with our reality. Awareness includes understanding intimately how your body moves within its environment. How far can we jump? How fast can we run? How high can we climb? Historically we learned these things as children in the simple pleasures of play. Now we watch 'ourselves' do these things as part of a video game. In this we move farther away from reality instead of closer to it. To accomplish strong magic (i.e. manipulate reality) we must immerse ourselves in that reality.

 Practice Six

Our skin is the largest sense organ of our bodies. Touch is the first sense experienced by a baby and the last sense to fade away. Yet we are taught from babyhood to cover this sense organ up, cutting ourselves off from much of the input we might otherwise add to experience.

- Go to a well-tended garden. Dig your hands into the soft earth. Feel the consistency of that earth. Smell it. Taste it. Go to a vacant lot and do the same. Farmers for thousands of years could distinguish good growing soil from poor and tell what crops would do well in a given area with no more testing than this.
- Gently rub your face with both hands. How does this sensation feel to your face? How does it feel to your hands? Both sensations are yours, how are they connected?
- Get two small pieces of sandstone. Grip them tightly in your hand. How do they feel? How does your hand feel gripping something? Grind the two pieces of stone together / crush them for a moment. How does the feeling change as they change from rocks to sand?
- On a warm day find a small hill covered with grass. Wear as little as practical (and legal). Lie down on the grass and roll down the hill. How does it feel? Can you feel each blade of grass as it touches you? At the bottom of the hill simply sit for a moment. How long does the feeling from the grass last? What does the absence of the feeling of the grass feel like?

Experiment with feeling, not only when you touch something but also when something touches you. You may find closing your eyes will help you focus on feeling.

 ## *Practice Seven*

One gets the feeling sometimes that before the invention of clocks no one was ever able to wake up on time or coordinate actions for a group over time. I'm not sure this is true. Within our dimension the time arrow moves in one direction only (forward). As we are part of this universe we are innately attached to a sense of time. However, most of us never develop that sense, relying on mechanical devices to tell time for us instead. Time can be broken down to specific points (e.g. 10:00) and durations (e.g. 1 ½ hours).

- Before you go to sleep tell yourself three times to wake up 5 minutes (e.g. 6:25 AM) before your alarm is set to go off (e.g. 6:30 AM). Do this for 10 days in a row. It isn't really important whether you wake up exactly 5 minutes early or not (although if you do, great). What's more important is you'll probably find you wake up close to the same number of minutes early each day. This is your natural offset. With practice you can use this as a personal alarm clock by simply telling yourself three times what time you need to awaken and you'll wake up a bit before that time.

- Get a watch with a second hand. Pick a starting point and when the second hand passes that point close your eyes. Without counting the seconds simply wait until you feel one minute has passed. Open your eyes and check the time. How many seconds passed? Do several trials. Do not try to modify your behavior to better tell when a minute has passed. Instead simply wait until you feel one minute has passed. You probably will find the number of seconds that pass within your feeling is fairly constant. This number is your 'short time'. Do the same practice using 15 minutes as the time interval. The number you come up with is your 'long time'. With practice you should be able to combine your long times and short times to create almost any time interval. Folks that use this are remarkably accurate in judging how much time has passed between two events.

 ## Practice Eight

To take awareness to the next level, combine stillness with all your senses. Become still and then immerse your senses in your environment. Do not seek to single out any particular sight / sound / feeling. Instead be aware of the gestalt. Seek to experience the overall vibration of your environment. Try to find its balance and how that balance changes over time. Work to refine your ability to sense the vibration of things. One must be able to sense vibrations to be able to synchronize with them and to alter their power, flow, direction and structure. This ability is critical to succeed in both physical and metaphysical endeavors. We'll revisit this in the chapter on Magical Ritual.

Memory

The first mental ability we developed as organisms was the ability to remember things. Memory had a huge impact on our ability to survive. Being able to remember where food might be found, what kind of animals might try to eat us, where we could hide or be safe was all critical information in the day to day activities of staying alive. The better we became at remembering vis-à-vis other animals, the more we gained ascendancy in the food chain.

Over time, having memory enabled us to learn to communicate with others in complex ways. To increase the persistence of individual memory we began to move our memories to the group via the telling of stories. This enabled the group to remember things longer than the lifetime of the individual (which at that time was usually painfully short), as well as facilitated building our shared reality.

As story tellers and the keepers of the group memory, bards, monks and wise men learned to remember thousands of pages of information they then could retrieve verbatim upon demand. However, this was a lot of work, required special training, and few had a talent for it. Additionally, it carried a high risk in that if the bard was killed or suddenly died then the group stood a chance of losing access to the group memory. Thus, a more general and more accessible form of group memory was needed. So we invented means of artificial memory, first as writing / printing and, in modern times, through a variety of devices (e.g. disk storage, DVD, flash memory).

The issue is the ability to remember, like any other skill, requires use to maintain its sharpness. We have grown so reliant upon the use of artificial memory that we've allow our own innate abilities to atrophy. Instead of being able to easily recall thousands of pages of information on demand, we now struggle to remember the two pages necessary to give a speech. We can be rendered helpless by the simple event of not having an extra battery.

As an exercise, get a piece of paper and write down a detailed description of a loved one's face. Obviously, if you have a deep affection for someone, you should be able to, at least, give the police a good description of your loved one should she suddenly go missing.

Similarly, write down a fairly detailed description of your day yesterday. For example, you may be able to remember what you had for lunch, but do you remember what color the plate it was served on was? Some may bring up they don't remember because such stuff is simply trivia and they have far more important things to remember. This argument is fair enough. However, to test its validity, pick some set of recurring events that you deem important and describe in detail the time before the time before last, not just who was there but what they were wearing, what they said and what they did. Impossible? Not really.

Science has found that you store EVERY experience that you have ever had, although over time the chemical connections do break down (i.e. the memories become fuzzier). Brain surgeons have documented that, upon physical stimulation to certain areas of the brain, patients will claim to be 'reliving' experiences in their pasts.

Our inability to remember doesn't stem from some modern affliction. What is probably more correct is we rarely structure information to make it easy to remember, take the time to ensure we focus enough to remember it and maintain the pathways necessary to access and retrieve the information we have.

We need a better balance between what we carry around in our own memories versus what we offload to external artificial memories. In doing magic it's very difficult, and sometimes dangerous, to interrupt an activity / ritual to thumb through a grimoire (heaven forefend booting up a computer). Additionally, we run the risk of losing access to important things due to the artificial storage being destroyed or simply inaccessible when needed.

Awareness enables access to the physical and metaphysical worlds. Memory enables persistent access to that awareness and the ability to later reflect upon one's experience to better understand that experience instead of only relying on our impressions in the moment. Awareness and Memory are key components needed for Visualization, which is critical to doing strong magic. Last, for most of us, as we age our ability to remember tends to get worse. Thus it's important to 'use it or lose it'.

In this chapter we'll learn how to remember better and recall more easily. It might even help you find your cell phone upon occasion.

The ability to remember can be broken down into three steps:

- Acquisition
- Storage
- Retrieval

We have two types of memory: short term and long term. These are not sharply defined where a particular memory can only be one or the other (the digital world) but tend to merge into each other depending on the situation. (As a side note, learning can be defined as the act of moving information from short term memory to long term memory, so improving this transfer has the added benefit of increasing your ability to learn more quickly and easily.)

Many people complain of having a poor memory when it's really being overwhelmed with information that is causing their inability to remember. The first step in being able to remember is to acquire the information. This needs:

- Awareness
- Attention
- Organization / Formatting
- Moving data / information into memory

Before you can remember something you must elevate its status to something you want to remember and then take time to create a memory. Although this sounds like a lot of work, after a little practice it becomes automatic.

Folks sometimes ask me for my phone number. I tell them I don't remember it because I never call me. However, if they ask for my wife's phone number I rattle it off with ease. The difference is that I need to call my wife frequently so I've taken the time to learn (create a memory of) her phone number. It wasn't particularly difficult, but I did have to focus my attention and repeat her phone number a few times to move it into my long term storage. Focusing attention on the thing to be remembered is the second step.

This simple approach, becoming aware of needing to remember something, focusing your attention on it for a short time and repeating it a few times to capture it as a memory works for simple things but breaks down quickly as things become more complex.

The third step is to take time to organize / format what you want to remember not only to make it easier to commit to memory but easier to retrieve it at a later time. To understand how this is done takes a short foray into how your memory works.

When you create a memory your brain creates a series of electrochemical bonds which, subsequently, your brain can decipher into the original information when you want to recall it. The more times you reinforce the memory the more chemicals are laid down and the stronger the memory becomes. This is why rote memorization (simple repetition of something until it's remembered) works. However, this approach quickly becomes both time consuming and cumbersome.

The second aid to remembering is the more senses you use in creating the memory, the more chemicals are laid down and the stronger the memory becomes.

The third aid to remembering is information is far easier to recall if it's organized in such a way to facilitate retrieval.

The objective of memory is the ability to RECALL information quickly and clearly, not just to have a lot of stuff stored away. For the long term, organizing / formatting memory is the most important thing to achieving consistent recall.

To illustrate, perhaps you studied mathematics in school. If so, you probably encountered the approach where you were taught a lot of stuff about Algebra and then a lot of stuff about Geometry and then a lot of stuff about Trigonometry and finally some stuff about Calculus. You probably did well at first in Algebra and Geometry but rapidly lost interest because the stuff you were being shown didn't seem to have much importance or application in the real world. The outcome of this was by the time you got into Trigonometry and Calculus you had 'forgotten' (actually never learned) the stuff you were exposed to in Algebra and Geometry that's necessary to learn Trigonometry and Calculus, making it such a burden to learn these new topics that you gave up on math as generally just a bad idea and moved on to easier topics you found more interesting.

Let's wind the clock forward several years and you now want to landscape your backyard so it will be a really nice place for your kids to play in and to sit around with your friends on weekends. You decide to do a little research on how best to do the landscaping so you don't waste your hard earned money by making mistakes.

New concepts like the need for proper drainage show up with diagrams (geometry and trigonometry) and formulas (algebra) attached. What you've just discovered was these mathematical disciplines were originally worked out so people could DO something (like build the pyramids, sail ships, and dig irrigation canals).

Having a practical objective gives focus to the math but also utilizes only the portion of each type of mathematics necessary to achieve the objective.

The common approach of teaching each branch of mathematics as a separate piece may make them easier to teach but probably makes them significantly harder to learn and isn't the way most people actually use mathematics.

The more we can personalize information (i.e. tie it to something we find important, format it in the way we view the universe) the easier it is to remember. Learning about tangents may not seem important but keeping water from flooding the basement does.

This integration into our world view takes time and effort. The benefit is what we learn in this way we rarely forget. People say that older people learn more slowly than young people. It may be more correct to say older people learn differently than young people.

The young are more willing to memorize factoids because it is the way they are taught in school. Having developed a world view over time, older people are more concerned with how new information fits into that world view and its usefulness. The tradeoff is young people tend to forget things just as easily as they learn them whereas older people learn more slowly but retain what they learn longer.

It's also important to understand how we learn certain things. People say young people learn languages easier than older people. This is usually true but why? One reason is that learning a language is a right brain activity while speaking a language is a left brain activity. When coupled with a willingness to memorize factoids (e.g. vocabulary lists) without immediately trying to integrate the information, young people have the edge in learning languages. This is why modern language teaching methods use a variety of tricks to get the student to kick their left brain out of gear and let the right brain engage.

Finally, as memory is a physical function (creating chemical bonds) as well as a mental one, our physical condition affects how well we can remember. Stress, poor diet, poor physical condition and poor health all negatively impact our memory. The mind and body are not separate but are one, and both should be kept in good shape.

Organizing and formatting the information to be stored greatly facilitates our ability to move it from short term to long term memory. Several methods to do this have been developed over the years. Each one tends to work better than the others in specific scenarios. As with meditative methods, you'll probably find that some work better than others for you.

Although it may seem like a lot of trouble, take the time to work through each practice. Limiting the amount of information you work with will speed things up, but use enough complexity to gain an understanding of each technique.

As mentioned above, people rarely take the time to actually work at remembering things. The pace of modern living coupled with people living significantly longer has moved having a bad memory from a minor inconvenience to a functional impediment, especially as memory tends to naturally degrade with age. The techniques below have been proven to work. Once learned, they can be mixed and matched to fit the demands of the moment. In learning them you'll come to understand what kinds of information you remember easily and what kinds you don't. When faced with the latter, you'll know to take extra time to move important information to long term memory, so it will be there when needed.

 Practice One

The first approach is to create a **list** of the items to be remembered. Folks commonly do this before going to the grocery store (and then promptly forget several things on the list). Formatting the list into groups with common themes (e.g. all fruits together, all boxed items together, all green things together) or that you can add an association to (e.g. all the stuff you hate to eat but is good for you, all the stuff you love to eat but really can't afford) will help your memory.

Have someone create a list with twenty items. Items on the list should be random. Look at the list for a minute (roughly 3 seconds per item) and then put the list away. Write down on a piece of paper as many of the items as you can recall.

Have someone create a list of twenty items that have strong similarities and can be broken down into 4 distinct groups (5 items in each group). Look at the list for roughly a minute and then put the list away. Write down on a piece of paper as many of the items as you can recall. Which approach worked better for you?

Adding meta-data about the list to your memory also helps. For example, knowing each group above has five items in it can help trigger connections. You may forget one item each in two groups on the first pass but then can remember them by focusing on each group one at a time and thinking about what item is missing.

 ## Practice Two

Association is the next approach. By linking items to something that can be sensed or mentally attached to each item helps your memory. This is one way folks are taught to remember people's names. Just being introduced to Joe as one of a crowd won't help you remember his name but noticing Joe has really big ears and remembering 'Big Eared Joe' will probably stick his name in your mind.

The next time you are at a gathering make it a point to pick out some distinctive feature or attribute for each of the first ten people you meet. Wait for a time and then, before people leave, look at each person and recall each one's name.

Similarly, pick out a food you love to make. The next time you have it take the time to sense it. Associate its sense memory with each of its ingredients and fairly quickly you won't need a cookbook anymore. For example, pumpkin pie is made with milk, eggs, pumpkin, cinnamon, allspice, ginger and salt, and has a distinctive smell, taste and texture. If any of the ingredients are left out or are out of proportion, the mixture simply doesn't look, smell or taste 'right'. This also helps build awareness by causing you to pick out what foods are made of rather than just their gestalt.

 ## Practice Three

Inner stories / movies can be used to capture details as well as actions. Start at your front door and walk through two or three rooms in your house. Pretend that your eyes are a movie camera and pan the camera slowly around the room, taking note of the items in the room in detail as you walk through it. When done sit down somewhere else in your house and play the movie in your mind. Write down all the things you noticed AND their spatial relationship to one another (e.g. The five foot lamp with the beige shade is in the left corner of the living room. The lamp is next to the table with the red rose in the white bud vase. My reading glasses and the book "Quantum Magic" are also on top of the table next to the right side of the vase. The table is next to left side of the brown overstuffed recliner chair with the small, green and white striped throw blanket draped on the back).

Next, pick a day where you will be engaged in a variety of activities. As you go through the day make up a story about what is happening. It's fine to embellish the story with fanciful details if you wish.

For example, our hero Lance Sterling got out of bed at 6:00 AM on Thursday. This was notable because Lance made it a point never to get out of bed before 6:30 on Thursdays. He wondered all the way through his breakfast of eggs, bacon and toast what could possibly have gone awry with his carefully engrained habit. After breakfast he got on his trusty steed Mustang, which he had purchased several years before in a nearby village from Mr. Ford. Lance didn't look forward to the day because he knew he would have to deal with the evil Overlord 'Boss'...

Wait for a week and remember your story. Could you write down a list of your activities for that day using it?

 Practice Four

Rhymes have been used for thousands of years as a mechanism to aid memory. Many spells are specifically rhymed to help the practitioner remember a sequence of activities or the ingredients needed to accomplish a particular piece of magic.

As an example:

> High John and Lily Constancy
> Happy, they wished to be
> Devil's Milk and Lady's Meat
> Help make a white sachet complete
> If the Meadow Lady can be found
> Mountain Joy comes around
> If woe there be still to fix
> Add some Trumpet Weed to the mix

Translation:

To promote happiness make a small pouch (sachet) of white cloth. Within it place the following ingredients: High John the Conqueror (High John), Lily of the Valley (Lily Constancy), Celandine (Devil's Milk), Hawthorn (Lady's Meat), Meadowsweet (Lady of the Mountain), Marjoram (Joy of the Mountain) and Morning Glory (Trumpet Weed). The pouch can then be worn or placed inside the home.

Make a short list of activities or items that you find hard to remember. Create a rhyme using the list. Does the rhyme help you remember?

 Practice Five

Cascades are like tables of organization and work well for information that easily fits into a hierarchical format.

In olden times some tribes' rememberers would 'name' each year for an important event that occurred during the year (e.g. the year of the great flood, the year the war ended). The name would be the trigger for all of the memories for that year, allowing, for example, everything to be broken down to events before, during and after the named event.

Another example is remembering a family tree. Some cultures have a heavy emphasis on knowing all the names and relationships of one's extended family, sometimes encompassing several dozen or even hundreds of people. <u>Cascade memory</u> (e.g. everyone in Mother's family, then their children, then their grandchildren) puts this information in a good format to remember.

Cascades don't work as well for information that is heavily inter-related and can't be easily compartmentalized. Math, as mentioned above, is rarely used one topic at a time, even though it's taught that way. Thus, even though it might seem logical to group math into a cascade, it makes it very hard to remember.

Pick something that has a lot of items and can be grouped easily (e.g. your family tree, the books in your library). Create a tree chart for the information and start memorizing it from the top level downward to the bottom. As you change levels, be sure you've gotten the level above correct. This aids in recreating the chart because if you know the third level has eight items but can only recall six, you may remember items in the next layer down that will help recall the missing pieces. Don't be concerned with any interrelationships between items. That kind of scenario is addressed below under networks.

(As a side note, organizing items into categories that aren't readily apparent may help you to recall things but confuse other people. For example, if you don't like people messing up your books, you might arrange them so all the green ones are together, and the brown ones and the blue ones… It's sometimes why folks say "I know exactly where everything is.", even though no one else does.)

 Practice Six

Networks are much better suited to capturing interrelationships in information and is the way your brain tends to connect things. Networks are formed by connecting a set of nodes together. A common example of this is your 'network' of friends. You know Adam, Beth, Chuck and Debbie. Adam knows you, Beth and Debbie but not Chuck. Beth knows you, Adam and Chuck but not Debbie. Chuck knows you and Beth but neither Debbie nor Adam. Debbie knows you and Adam but neither Beth nor Chuck. Perhaps a network diagram shows it better:

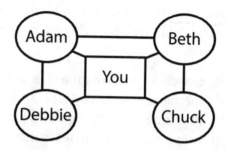

That is why formatting this kind of information in a network diagram makes it easier to remember. The graphic presents all of the data as a gestalt which can be remembered as one thing not many things (a picture is worth a thousand words). This particular diagram could be remembered as a pyramid with you at the top and your four friends at each corner. The lines from each person's circle shows whom they know. The bottom line of the pyramid (between Debbie and Chuck) is missing because they don't know each other.

An important attribute to networks is they can be self-healing (resilient) because, in the same way black holes were discovered, the connections can be used to deduce what the missing information must be to make the connections whole again.

Pick a craft you know a lot about. Make a list of the basic techniques that are used over and over (i.e. the 20% of the techniques that are used in 80% of the work). Create a network diagram with those techniques as the nodes. Connect the nodes with different colored lines depending on which techniques are combined to create certain items within the craft. For example, in cooking one can Braise, Broil, Fry, Grill, Poach, Roast, Sauté, Steam, and Stew, but the Network Node should be the more Meta 'Heat'. Make an index that shows what can be made using each color's nodes.

Practice Seven

Mnemonics are acronyms, words, phrases that help us to remember. Common mnemonics are:

- 'Every Good Boy Deserves Favor' (EGBDF) is a mnemonic for the treble clef used in writing music.
- 'My Very Elderly Mother Just Sat on Uncle Ned's Parrot' (Mercury, Venus, Earth, Mars, Jupiter, Saturn, Uranus, Neptune, Pluto) is a mnemonic for the planets (as well as having a strong visual component that aids in remembering).
- 'Tanstaafl' (There Ain't No Such Thing As A Free Lunch) is something many folks tend to forget, especially when the government is involved, or magicians when they think they can get something for nothing simply by using magic.

Pick a set of seven things or less. Take the first letter of the name of each item and try to arrange them into a word or something that creates an association for you (e.g. SCUBA (Self Contained Underwater Breathing Apparatus), TEAPOTS (Title Eight Automated Paperless Office Tracking System) or CIA WTF (the Central Intelligence Agency's WikiLeaks Task Force)). Sometimes a vowel needs to be added to make the word complete. In that case the mnemonic is written in capital letters and the added vowels in small letters. *AACR TWFTJ TJW SWNE ToT*

Pick a set of seven things or less. Take the first letter of the name of each item and try to come up with words beginning with those letters that create a coherent, and easily remembered sentence.

 Practice Eight

Memory has an interesting constraint in that the mind has difficulty remembering more than seven items at a time. One of the reasons there was lots of consternation when the phone company added requiring area codes to the dialing of phone numbers (ten numbers instead of seven). A more interesting attribute is the mind doesn't seem to care how many things are within each item. **Chunking** is deliberately taking many things, putting them into related groups and then remembering them as one 'chunk.'

Have someone put ten objects on a table and cover them with a cloth. Take the cloth away for 30 seconds and study the objects. Re-cover the objects. Write down the objects you can remember. (If this is too easy, add objects and/or reduce the viewing time.)

Have someone put ten different objects on a table and cover them with a cloth. Take the cloth away but this time try to see the table top as one photograph. After 10 seconds, replace the cloth and write down the objects you can remember. With practice you should be able to remember 'tens' of objects after only the second or two it takes to create the 'snapshot'.

 Practice Nine

The last technique we'll explore is the creation of your own knowledge 'library.' The original application of this technique involved creating a large room full of card files. Within each card file was a series of cards with a 'factoid' on each one. When one needed to know something, he/she visualized entering the library, going to the card file, pulling the appropriate card and 'reading' the factoid.

Now-a-days we have the ability to visualize a much more modern and well-appointed library which can include such wonders as holographic images, interconnected media (e.g. videos, audios, text / diagrams, images). The size and complexity of your library is only limited by your imagination and your ability to visualize.

As this practice initially can be very time consuming and requires a lot of work, pick a very limited subject of continued interest for you (something you'd really like to remember for a long time). First decide what your library will look like and how it will be arranged. Use all of the techniques mentioned above to format all of the information you know about the subject. Pick the best way to present the information back to you (e.g. sometimes a movie, sometimes a graphic, sometimes a 'sense-o-gram'). The presentation medium can be anything you can imagine. The objective is to make each item as informationally 'dense' as possible.

When done, begin a meditation to sensorially create your library. Make it spacious with plenty of room for storage and expansion. Visualize yourself going to the area you've chosen to store your target subject. Visualize placing the information is its proper place with everything needed to access it near at hand. Leave your library, actively remembering the pathway to the information. End the meditation.

At first this probably will seem to be an awful lot of trouble, but it becomes easier with practice until it ultimately is simply the way you remember things. The payoff is it creates a way that you can remember virtually everything that you feel important to remember, in any level of detail you choose, for as long as you want to remember it.

***

A few final words about memory / learning. In many fields, imparting information is done by factoid, a lot of discrete bits of information without any framework to hang them on. One is supposed to somehow just discover the framework over time (usually leading to an epiphany when a lot of stuff that one has struggled with for a long time simply becomes clear).

This approach is not only very frustrating to the learner but inefficient as well. Repetition (Rote Memorization), Lists, Rhymes and Mnemonics aid in retaining factoids. The more complex and powerful methods (i.e. Cascades, Networks) require a framework (Meta) approach to work well. How well one constructs the framework directly affects how easily the information is stored, retrieved and understood.

Frameworks tend to be simple (even simplistic) and straight forward. For example, to build a simple house basically one needs to know how to build a wall with a hole in it. A ceiling or floor is a wall laid flat. A roof is a wall laid at an angle. A door or window or staircase requires a hole in the wall. A foundation is a really thick and strong wall.

Unfortunately, one usually needs a broad and deep understanding of a subject to see what the underlying framework must look like. One of the functions of a Master was to provide that framework to the Apprentice and the Craftsman, and the ability to do so was the primary distinction between a Master and a Craftsman.

An Apprentice focuses on answering what needs to be done, how and by whom. A Craftsman focuses on answering where and when it needs to be done. The Master knows WHY it should be done. Answering 'why' is a good way to capture a subject's Meta data and understand its underlying framework, which, in turn, creates the Cascade or Network needed to remember lots of complex information over time.

Last, be sensitive to the blessing of forgetfulness. Some believe that we should remember everything because the reality of life is it contains pleasure and pain, good times and bad, and so on. While true, this truth can hinder folks from ever becoming content with their lot, much less find happiness or enduring joy. Sometimes it is right, while still learning from experience, to lay bad experiences to rest and leave their baggage behind. Sometimes it is best to go into your library and throw a memory out with the trash, to simply forget. As has been said, "Write bad things in sand, carve good things in stone."

Focus / Concentration

Focus / concentration is sometimes called 'attention span'. Most adults can focus on one thing for only around 5 to 20 minutes. Some folk's attention span lasts for only a few seconds. Focusing on one thing shouldn't be confused with focusing on something for a short time and then re-focusing on the same thing for another short time. (This has become known as 'multitasking'.) Many magical endeavors require deep and sustained attention measured in hours, sometimes days, not minutes or seconds. Thus, developing the ability to keep focused is a critical skill to success.

If you have been working on the practices in the previous chapters then the first step for focusing should be relatively easy: clear your mind and find stillness. The second step may still need work: the ability to consistently ignore distractions and remain in the stillness.

One of the most distracting things in our high pressure lives is the constant focus on time. Everything is supposed to be done instantaneously because we always have 'something else to do'. Magical practice was developed in an earlier, slower paced time when the extreme drive to always be actively doing something was not the norm. Additionally, those activities that taught concepts like patience are no longer done by most folks.

To illustrate, hunting requires patience. Non-hunters quickly become agitated when required to simply be quiet and motionless. They frequently will ask the guide / hunter, "shouldn't we be doing something?" To this question the guide will frequently respond, "We are doing something; we're waiting." A way to resolve this dilemma is to actively 'gather patience.'

Achieving stillness and then removing distractions creates the mental workspace necessary to maintain concentrated effort, to immerse one's self in the moment of the task or activity.

There's a story of a king who wanted to ensure the suitors of his daughter had the right qualifications, one of which was coolness in stressful situations. He created a test where the suitor had to walk along a narrow beam over an abyss while all sorts of distractions (e.g. fire erupting, arrows flying past, sudden loud noises) happened. The task was simple: the person had to walk the beam while carrying a full cup of tea to the king's daughter and complete this task without spilling a drop. So many tried and failed the king was about to give up, when the court fool asked to try. To everyone's amazement the fool was successful. When asked how this was possible, the fool simply said "I was too busy trying not to spill that damned tea to pay attention to anything else."

Developing focused attention is best accomplished by engaging in things that require it, and this requires a willingness to break out of the current habits of multitasking and being satisfied with superficial results quickly and easily obtained. It resurrects concepts like: craftsmanship, thoughtfulness, excellence, and so forth, qualities that many times require a lifetime of work and learning the 80% of the skills that are only used 20% of the time. That is, becoming truly competent at the 'craft' of something.

Accomplishing this in any one activity teaches a way of doing things that can be easily transferred to other endeavors because it becomes simply the way one approaches life and ceases to be anything special.

A common theme today is "I'm never going to be world class at this, so why should I put in a lot of effort doing it when it's so much easier to simply buy the product / service from someone who is world class?"

Developing the skills in this book isn't about comparing yourself to others or beating someone in a competition. It is about becoming all you can be, both magically and personally. Developing focus isn't really about reaching a goal but engaging in a lifelong pursuit. For most, the path to mastering skills is hard and long, but the rewards are well worth the journey. Success is measured by being better today than you were yesterday. It is a process rather than a destination.

Practice One

Pick a game that requires using awareness, memory and concentration. A game that has many ways to play and win. Chess is a good example, Bridge another. Most video games are not because winning can be achieved many times through simply remembering the actions necessary to get through each level. Few video games change what needs to be done to pass a level one session to the next.

After learning the basics, first determine what the true objective of the game is. What does it take to win? For example, in Poker most think the objective is to win the most hands when, in fact, the objective is to end up with the most money at the end of the game. This changes the way one plays the game significantly by adding a focus on betting strategies to that of playing strategies.

Next take time to learn the impacts of doing certain moves or employing certain tactics. In Chess, for example, seizing the center of the board versus using flanking attacks from the sides. Take the time to think through where each action will likely lead and what results are likely to be gained from one approach over another before making a move. That is, learn the basic winning strategies of the game.

Last become aware that playing the game doesn't occur in a vacuum. Usually at least one other person (your opponent) is involved and, thus, the game occurs against a social backdrop. This may lead to a more nuanced idea of what constitutes winning. For example, when teaching, always besting your apprentice simply because you can may not be the best way for the apprentice to learn.

Similarly, Tic-Tac-Toe is a very simple game that teaches basic military strategy. Fairly quickly one learns that by consistently using a very few responses the result is always a 'cat' game (i.e. no winner). Perhaps the hidden lesson is that no one really ever wins a war, and the only logical thing to do is not play.

Practice Two

Pick a sport / activity that is highly dynamic and highly variable. Look for something that requires making a lot of decisions quickly and having to consistently adapt to changing circumstances. Martial arts is a good example, whereas most kinds of dance are not. These kinds of activities require one to be 'in the moment' to succeed. To stay in the moment requires a great deal of focus. Video games can be a choice here, so long as you haven't played the game so much that you simply are going through the same motions rather than having to truly engage in playing the game.

 ## *Practice Three*

Pick a craft, almost any of them will do. Take the time to become really good at it. How will you know when you're good at it? By being able to look at something you've created (which doesn't have to be fancy or ornate) and being able to truthfully say to yourself, "Look at that. It is well done."

Most crafts require a degree of creativity as well as skill. Creativity many times requires the ability to visualize the result. Leading us to the next chapter.

Visualization

Awareness, memory and focus come together in building visualizations. The ability to create and maintain visualizations (perhaps more correctly sensationalizations) is crucial to doing strong magic.

The more senses you can engage in the visualization, the more 'real' it becomes. The principles of visualization are well known and used successfully in many different venues. They are taught at the Olympic Center to world class athletes, in seminars to business leaders, in many self-help books, and so forth.

Magical ritual requires accessing energy, channeling / focusing that energy into a purpose, manifesting it in our reality and then releasing it to accomplish the desired goal (more on this in the chapters on Magic and Magical Ritual). Good visualization skills greatly improve the quality of each of those steps.

Additionally, in group work the better each person can participate in creating and maintaining the visualization, the stronger the shared reality will be, the more synchronized the energy will be and the more powerful the spell will be.

Perhaps the most commonly experienced altered state of consciousness is dreaming. All people dream, although many don't remember their dreams. You should begin a dream diary to record your dreams, for, in most cases, they will quickly fade from your memory.

Most dreams are just random firings of electrical impulses and don't have any real meanings. Some dreams are the subconscious 'making sense of the day' or trying to resolve a thorny issue. In some dreams you may be aware that you're dreaming (called lucid dreaming). While most people usually dream in black and white, sometimes a dream may be in color and can include more senses than just sight (called vivid dreaming). Last, upon occasion you may experience something that feels like a dream but, in fact, is an altered state of consciousness. A doorway into other realities. Vivid dreaming is an easy frame of reference for creating visualizations because they are so real while being experienced.

The more vivid / detailed you can make your visualization, the more senses you can engage in it, the more memorable you can make it, the more powerful it will be and the easier it will be for you to immerse yourself in it. Unfortunately, it is also easier for you to find discrepancies and have it fall to pieces.

Building a good visualization is like writing a good story. Some people like to build their visualizations a layer at a time, beginning with something simple and then adding detail and nuance bit by bit in a fairly structured way. Others tend to go with the flow and notice things along the way, a smell here, a view there, exploring their visualization and discovering its detail and nuance.

Don't try to force visualizations as doing so tends to be counterproductive. Over time you'll find what approaches work best for you. Be creative in your approaches.

 Practice One

Get a mirror (some prefer to use a black scrying mirror rather than the more conventional reflective kind). See yourself in the mirror. Now visualize yourself regressing to a younger and younger age. See yourself becoming younger, manipulating your time sense. As an aid, take a look at pictures of yourself throughout your past to help you build the visualization.

Once mastered, the next step is to visualize how you will look in the future, aging yourself. This is usually more difficult as folks tend to shy away from how they will really look and wind up with just adding a wrinkle or two. The closer visualizations are to reality the more powerful they are. The 'truer' they are. Unfortunately sometimes the truth can be quite uncomfortable.

When moving your image back and forth in time is working reasonably well, add other senses. How did you feel (kinesthetic sense) when young? How will you feel when old? Make your visualization more detailed and more nuanced.

 Practice Two

In the chapter on memory you built your library. Now is the time to build your sanctuary. Your sanctuary is a place you can always go to rest and recuperate from the stresses of this reality or contemplate on the meaning of things. You can visit it any time and stay as long as you like. It's important to understand your sanctuary is a place to rest not retreat. We exist in this reality, and it's important to learn ways to cope with it. Running away from it (living in your mind) by staying in your sanctuary for long periods of time as a way of avoiding life is not only counterproductive but significantly limits your ability to learn the lessons of life / reach enlightenment.

As we are unique, each person's sanctuary will also be unique. Only you can decide what it looks like, how it is laid out inside and what environment it exists within. You may want to start with your library and create the place within which it resides. Or you may want to create your sanctuary as a separate place that is very different in aspect from your library. The good news is your sanctuary can be changed easily as you find your needs change. It is a place that can consistently be 'under construction'. Thus, begin small and leave plenty of room for growth.

As examples, one sanctuary might be a large modernistic building filled with gadgets, while another might be a nice dry cave with lots of winding passage ways leading to rooms and caverns filled with esoteric treasures, while another might simply be a nice glade with old trees and a stream. Your sanctuary is only limited by your imagination, creativity and your ability to visualize it in detail. As you become better at visualization, you can make your sanctuary more secure and stronger also.

The last step is to create a distinctive and memorable path you'll use to reach your sanctuary. This might be a doorway marked in some special way, a pathway through a familiar place (e.g. a wood, a meadow) or a transportation device (e.g. a ship, a transporter).

Whatever the mechanism, it's important to know and understand it from both sides (what it looks like going to and coming from your sanctuary). An experience many children have is having a 'secret' place only to lose the ability to go there as they grow up because they can no longer seem to find the secret door or passage that leads them there. Losing at the same time the refuge that significantly helps one deal with the stresses of the world.

Developing strong awareness, memory, concentration and visualization skills enables one to do powerful magic. This is not to be confused with traveling to esoteric realms, engaging in psychic activities or experiencing altered states of consciousness, which are somewhat existent independent of the practitioner.

Visualization can be misused to create a more pleasant / pleasurable place than one finds oneself in in this reality. A place one then uses to run away from life. Like taking a drug, it becomes easy to lose oneself in the experience. That path leads to madness.

Be sure not to go places you don't know how to return from. In a similar vein, never summon anything you don't know how to banish. These are real dangers with real consequences even if they 'only happen in your mind'. Be careful not to lose it. After all, it's the only one you have.

Magical vs. Psychic Abilities

Historically magical actions and psychic actions have been kept apart. They each have their own jargon, approaches and theories. However, the lines between them can blur a bit in practice, and their effects can look very much alike, even if the methods used to achieve those effects are very different.

Understanding the differences between magical and psychic abilities can help one know where his/her talents lie and changes what should be done to develop those talents. Additionally, psychic phenomena have been studied far more scientifically than magical phenomena and some of the methods used can be helpful to developing magical skill and vice-versa.

Even though the definitions are the same (a force or event not explainable by science or the accepted laws of nature), Paranormal is used when discussing psychic phenomena while Supernatural is used when discussing magical phenomena. The general feeling is magic is something you do while psychic is something you are and the way activities are broken down is quite different.

 Exercise One

Name the various common activities within magical and psychic studies. (Please do this before looking at the table on the next page.)

Magic	Psychic
Theurgy (working with gods)	Telepathy (mind to mind communication)
Thaumaturgy (wonder working/enchantment)	Psychokinesis / Levitation (moving things with one's mind)
Divination (future telling)	Clairsentience / Pre-cognition (future seeing / hearing / knowing)
Scrying (remote viewing/finding)	Remote Viewing (sensing information from a distance without pre-knowledge)
Invocation (allowing to enter)	Channeling (allowing one's self to be possessed by another)
Evocation (conjure / summon)	Aura Reading (sensing / interpreting a person's aura)
Banishing / Exorcism (forcing to leave)	Astral Travel / OOBE (spirit travel / out of body experiences)
Hexing / Cursing (breaking/causing harm)	Psychometry (sensing events by touching objects)
Healing	Teleportation (disappearing from one location and reappearing at a different location)
Binding	
Shielding	

Some of the categories blend into each other. For example, when a magician communicates with the gods is the mechanism used telepathy? Could someone become a better magician if they worked on becoming a better telepath? Would a talented telepath have a boost up in becoming a magician? Similarly, when a magician visits other worlds is the mechanism used astral travel? Is invoking a god a form of channeling?

A common model for telepathy is using the analogy of a radio. To establish a telepathic link one goes through a tuning or synchronization step to create the telepathic contact. The closer one is to the other's natural frequency the easier this step is to accomplish.

More metaphysically, some people are known to be more naturally sympathetic than others. As this ability strengthens, they become known to be empathic. As this ability strengthens, they become more telepathic. *turns* We hear of this with people who, usually after long acquaintance (synchronization), truly 'just know' what the other person is thinking.

Telepathic communication tends to be more graphic (using symbols, pictures) than word based. Thus, the sender needs to spend some time and effort in creating the mental image to be sent, and the receiver needs to spend some time and effort in understanding the nuances of the message received. As with Tarot cards, telepathic messages can be extremely information dense. Just as with a dream diary, this is one reason to write down, as quickly as possible, the message received before the details fade. This is especially true when dealing with entities not of this realm. It's very easy to misunderstand a message or miss something entirely due to not getting the details aright.

Zener cards (sometimes known as Rhine cards) have been used extensively in psychic research and have only five very basic shapes (circle, plus, square, star and three wavy vertical lines). Each of these graphics is very simple but would be difficult to confuse with any other of the graphics.

This model of telepathy ties in well with the magical vibrational / harmonizing / resonance model for communicating with other magical entities presented earlier. The use of graphical 'language' can explain why people don't have issues understanding other beings, as the 'textual' content is added by the receiver based upon their own frame of reference. It also explains why some communications might be fuzzy or have gaps, as the sender could be sending something for which the receiver has no frame of reference.

 Exercise Two

If you are an artist then draw the message below. If not, then map out textually what the message would look like. Both of these approaches are viable because the end result is a visualization. Whatever method you use is fine so long as you can use it to create a strong visual image.

If a picture is worth a thousand words then communicating graphically can be very information dense. Serious thought needs to be given to what will be included, how items will be positioned relative to other items, how pictures will be sequenced if there will be more than one (e.g. a storyboard approach), and so forth, to ensure the message is complete and not easily misunderstood.

This doesn't mean pictures must be extravagant or extremely detailed. Zen drawings are very simple and can use just a line to suggest a mountain or a stream. However, Zen drawings assume the viewer has the same frame of reference as the creator, which is less likely when dealing with supernatural beings. The trick is putting in enough detail without adding so much that the message becomes muddy or confusing.

The ability to think graphically has the additional benefits of enabling you to remember easier, to think faster, and, once you master the technique, to capture and understand significantly more detail from an experience.

Select a ritual that you recently performed or attended (or you can use the one in Chapter 12 (Creating and Performing Ritual)). Create a storyboard (a few to several pictures of events) that would communicate what happened at the ritual to another entity. A particularly difficult task is to communicate intention or the reasons something was done. Use the amount of detail in each picture that ensures the message is complete and difficult to misunderstand. Assume the receiver has some background in magical ritual and will understand the significance of certain artifacts (e.g. a cauldron, a candle, a pentagram) and how these artifacts are used within ritual.

When done, show the drawings / written text to your fellow magicians. Ask them to explain what they believe is being communicated and compare their explanation with what you intended to communicate (message sent versus message received).

This exercise has several magical and mundane benefits in that:

- It helps develop your ability to communicate clearly by driving home how easy it is to miscommunicate even simple messages.

- It helps develop your ability to get a message across with the minimum of content, enabling you to communicate more concisely.

- It helps develop your ability to select details to be included, and in what way, so as to increase informational content without increasing confusion.

- It helps develop your ability to visualize by giving you a stronger sense of how to build strong visualizations. This ability enables you to create stronger rituals and better guided meditations / visualizations for others.

Psychic phenomena tend to be human centric (e.g. dealings between humans alive or dead and phenomena in this reality only) while magical phenomena is not limited in that way (e.g. dealings with other kinds of entities and in other realities). This is a useful way to differentiate which skill set you're using.

In practice one should be sensitive to which skill set is being used. The way work is done and how skills can be developed are markedly different. Some things can be done far more easily using one approach over the other.

If you find you're psychic rather than magical, it probably would be better for you to switch tracks and study paranormal sources rather than magical ones.

Protocols and Practice

A complaint commonly voiced by non-magical folk is believers are simply engaging in 'wishful' thinking, as magic has never been proven to be true by science. Magical folk reply science has never proven magic to exist because scientists are simply too closed-minded to deal with anything that can't be measured in a laboratory.

Both positions may have some validity. Scientists spend a lot of effort differentiating between what is true, what might be true and what we would like to be true. So, magical folks probably could gain some value in adopting those scientific practices that could help them tell what's magically working and what is not.

However, these practices lose something in translation many times because scientific and magical folks tend to focus on different things and with different intensities. This harkens back to the earlier topics of perception, reality and the inter-relatedness of the multiverse.

As an illustration, magical folk are far more aware of, and put more credence in, synchronistic (meaningful coincidences) events. For example, you're unhappy at work, feeling trapped in your current job and so do a spell to have more happiness. A few days later an old friend calls that you haven't heard from for a long time and wants to have lunch with you and another friend. This lunch unexpectedly turns into a better job offer from the other friend. Coincidence or magic? A non-believer would usually say the former whereas magical folk the latter.

One of the differences in these realities is magical folk tend to have these 'coincidences' fairly frequently and come to look for and expect them. We are far more sensitive to fortuitous happenstances than our non-magical brethren, because magic is about changing probabilities and enhancing chances, not about turning the switch one way for a 1 and the other way for a 0.

We don't necessarily expect the results of our magic to be immediately apparent or immediately large. Frequently it takes some time for the results we want to manifest and sometimes we become aware that the manifestation occurred but not in the way we expected. This doesn't lend itself to the immediate cause and effect type of results non-believers tend to want.

However, perhaps a tighter connection between a magical action and its consequence can be observed by using the scientific idea of a 'protocol'.

A protocol is a series of steps specifically designed to ensure a result. In psychic research protocols were developed to ensure what was thought to be tested (hypothesis) was in fact what was tested.

For example, a person is supposed to do remote viewing. He/she is given information about what to work on and returns results to the examiner. But did the person actually engage in remote viewing, or did he use telepathy to read the expected results from the examiner's mind? What, in fact, was being observed?

To address this, the protocol calls for the information to be placed in a closed envelope so its contents will be unknown to the examiner. Because the examiner is 'blind' to the information, telepathy can be ruled out as a mechanism.

The following exercises are not meant to be scientifically rigorous but are to illustrate how psychic phenomena might be explored.

 Exercise One

Psychometry studies the ability of some people to describe past events by handling an object that was present at those events.

Get about a dozen people together, the more they are strangers to each other the better. Have them select a personal item that they were carrying during some recent significant event in their lives (e.g. car keys, a piece of jewelry). Each item should be passed around to each participant for evaluation. This takes a significant amount of time so leave ample time available. Don't rush.

Upon receiving an item, participants should:

- Take a moment to ground and center, specifically clearing their minds of any residual feelings from the previous object before they begin.

- Achieve stillness and open their awareness.

- Pick up the object and focus on letting it 'speak' to them. No expectations should be entertained. The person should simple note the feelings / impressions they receive without judging the validity or likelihood. Although this activity should not be rushed, sometimes a participant will simply get no impressions from an object and, after a reasonable time, should move on to the next one.

- Write down on a pad the impressions received.

- Put the object down for the next person to evaluate.

Given a dozen people, this generates 132 entries (11 X 12) to evaluate. The next step is to compare notes:

For each object, each person reads his/her impressions. The owner of the object does not offer any input until all others have spoken. Then the owner relates the event(s) that he/she was tying to the object.

What's being looked for is commonalities between evaluators' impressions and, as a separate category, congruence with the owner's event(s). The results don't have to be exact or match to the last detail. Close is good enough. The examiner should keep track of both statistics along with the names of the people (to be used in the next exercise).

Although the results of this exercise will be whatever they are, it's not unusual to get two or three people that will have the same impressions from a particular object and one to three people whose impressions match up with the actual events.

 Exercise Two

The results in the previous exercise could have been generated via psychometry, but they could also have been generated via telepathy. This exercise will use those results to explore telepathy.

For this exercise, the examiner should use the results from exercise one to pair an object's owner with people whose evaluation agreed with the owner's story of the events. (As the owner was busy evaluating objects while his/her object was being read, having the owner and evaluator agree is more likely due to psychometry.) Next, the people that agreed in their impressions but didn't agree with the owner should be paired (as these people agreed with each other but not the owner, telepathy may be more at work here). Pair any remaining participants together randomly.

Each person will have a chance to be a sender and a receiver (Sending: A-B, B-A). If more than two people are in a team then they should be set up as a round robin where each person acts as a sender and a receiver for every other person in the team. So a three member team will require six trials (Sending: A-B, A-C, B-A, B-C, C-A, C-B). This takes a significant amount of time. Don't rush.

The sender sits in a chair behind the receiver with both sender and receiver facing the same direction, so the receiver can't see the sender.

The sender should:

- Clear his/her mind and achieve stillness.
- Choose a simple action (e.g. scratch your head, stand up, look right) to communicate to the receiver. The sender should create a strong visual image of the receiver performing the action or an image that would cause the receiver to perform the action.

- Project this image to the receiver intensely for 20 – 30 seconds.

- Let the receiver know you've completed the sending.

The receiver should:

- Clear his/her mind and achieve stillness.

- Be aware and open to receiving the communication.

- If a strong urge to perform an action happens then do that action.

- If a feeling to do something occurs then note that feeling.

- Upon the sender signaling completion, the receiver should write down his/her impressions and feelings during the trial's time.

At the end of all the trials, participants should share their notes with the group, with the receiver relating their impressions first and then the sender relating their intent last (i.e. message received then message sent).

Although the results of this exercise will be whatever they are, it's not unusual to get one or two people who will perform the action that was requested telepathically and others who received a part of the message but it wasn't clear enough to act upon.

Even though these exercises are far from scientifically rigorous, getting any positive results would be interesting and probably indicate further research could be fruitful, as even two positive results in either exercise would exceed random chance.

Protocols can be adapted to magical practice to provide a more rigorous understanding of causal relationships. For example, synchronistic events usually come in multiples. One will note something that stands out and soon after something in the same theme will occur and then, perhaps, again, before the message will become clear. Writing down these occurrences when they happen provides a record of consistent experiences over time.

To illustrate, one record showed that when a person was extremely stressed and happened to drive down city streets at night, the streetlights would consistently go out (2 or 3 out of 10) for several blocks. This occurred for several weeks until the stress went away. When the stress went away the phenomenon also stopped. Some months later the same kind of situation occurred and the same phenomenon happened.

This same person found that when stressed and working out on an elliptical trainer with a heartrate monitor, the heartrate monitor would register his heartrate without him holding onto the handles or being connected in any way.

These experiences might have been caused by the person being able to generate a significant electrical field in some way. Obviously something was going on.

Using protocols has the added benefit of enabling you to learn what works for you and what doesn't, from technique, focus and magical approach standpoints. As with psychic phenomena, where one can be a wonderful psychometrician and a lousy telepath, magically one might be a very powerful thaumaturgist and a lousy diviner. Knowing your strengths and weaknesses is helpful in deciding how to improve your abilities.

Using protocols allows you to test what's happening and experiment with different approaches. By recording the results, patterns can be determined and then, based upon that knowledge, specific things can be developed to improve your potential as a practitioner.

Elemental Magic

To apply the skills we've learned we need to have a magical 'framework'. This framework enables us to select the skills to use, the ways to use them, and the order in which to use them in order to accomplish our magical goals.

Elemental magic is probably the oldest, if not the first, form of magic practiced by man. We are naturally attuned to elemental magic because we are made of and live with the elements from the beginning of our lives.

Although it can be simple, elemental magic is not necessarily simplistic as the elements can be combined in so many ways, some of which can be quite nuanced.

This simplicity reflects the physical world, where a few simple things are used in a large number of different combinations to create the universe. For example:

- All life on Earth is made from only four DNA components.
- Everything in the physical universe, through the process of fusion, comes from Hydrogen (the only element made up of the two (polarity, with only a proton and an electron and having no neutron)) and are combinations of roughly only 100 natural elements.
- There are only four mental states in humans: Delta, Theta, Alpha and Beta
    - Delta = 0.1 – 3 CPS (dreamless sleep, healing)
    - Theta = 3 – 7 CPS (deep meditation, dreaming)
    - Alpha = 7 – 13 CPS (alert meditation)
    - Beta = 13 – 30 CPS (external focus, awake state)

As a note: The Earth's vibration rate has been calculated as roughly 7.8 CPS (Alpha (alert meditation)) and people often say they feel most 'in tune' with the Earth while in this mental state.

For this primer, we'll use elemental magic as our framework due to its broad appeal. However, the skills learned through the previous work can be applied to any system. To develop this framework we need to have a 'language' (symbols, abstractions, connections) that facilitate our conceptualization and communication.

In the first chapter we learned the more tightly we can connect the physical with the metaphysical, the easier it is for us to visualize, energize and apply magic. There are many parallels within elemental magic and the physical world to make these connections.

State	Matter	Manifestation
Solid	Earth (sand, SiO_2)	Senses
Liquid	Water (H_2O)	Emotions
Energy	Fire (CH or $CHO_2 + O_2$)	Energizing Force
Gaseous	Air ($N + O$)	Intellect
Imagination	Spirit (O)	Creativity

Oxygen (chemical symbol: O) is the most abundant element in the Earth's crust (46%) with Silicon (Si) being the second most abundant. Thus, sand is an excellent magical reference for Earth, the primal force.

Hydrogen (H) is the primary and most abundant element in the universe and when combined with Oxygen yields Water, the life giver.

Carbon (C) is the basis of all earth type life when combined with Hydrogen to make organic chains (CH or CH + O2). When ignited in the presence of Oxygen organic material burns creating Fire, the transformer.

Nitrogen (N) is the most abundant element in the atmosphere (78%) and when combined with Oxygen, the 2nd most abundant element in the atmosphere (21%) makes 99% of what we call Air, the connector.

Oxygen is crucial to our very life's blood. The English word 'spirit' is derived from the Latin word for 'breath', and the breathing of Oxygen is required for us to sustain life. We can go without food for weeks, water for days, but without air we die within minutes. Thus, in the physical, Oxygen is in each of the four elements and unites them in the metaphysical with Spirit, the one.

 Exercise One

List the qualities you associate with each element with emphasis on the element's primal force. The list below enumerates some commonly held associations and can be used to give you a start. You may agree with some / all of them or have very different ideas. That's fine. What's important in this exercise is for you to start to attune yourself to the elements.

- Earth: potential energy, life, renewal / reuse, enduring, stability
- Water: flow, pressure, purification, dissolution, finding a way / level, smooth reaction
- Fire: energy, transformation, manifestation, dynamic power
- Air: communicative medium, connector, intellect, permeator
- Spirit: connectivity, linkage, oneness, creativity, direction

To Learn the Elements:

The craft of blacksmithing has always held an element of magic and the blacksmith held to have magical powers. Much can be learned of the elements, how they can be combined and how they interact, by the study of forging and blacksmithing. It is one of the few crafts that bring all of the elements together. *(ders.)*

Useful things come from the Earth (metal (inorganic) and coal (organic)) to make them, combined with Air and Fire to transform them, combined with Water to temper them and, finally, from the Spirit of the Smith, combining and binding the other elements into one, to create them.

The secrets of Iron, traditionally passed down from Master Smith to Craftsman to Apprentice, have many parallels to the passing down of magical knowledge, as well as the trials encountered in the learning of those secrets.

Being able to meditate on the elements is helpful to understand their attributes and powers. As learned earlier, sometimes having a focus aids in that meditation. A symbology to enable that focus can be putting the hands in a variety of positions that indicate each element.

 Exercise Two

Earth: Join the thumb and index (first) finger of your right hand into a circle. Interlock and join the thumb and index finger of your left hand into a circle with your right hand. Your right thumb should be on top of your left thumb. Extend the middle, ring and small fingers of both hands so they touch each other at the finger tips.

Water: Join the thumb and the middle (second) finger of your right hand into a circle. Interlock and join the thumb and middle finger of your left hand into a circle with your right hand. Your right thumb should be on top of your left thumb. Extend the index, ring and small fingers of both hands so they touch each other at the finger tips.

Fire: Join the thumb and the ring (third) finger of your right hand into a circle. Interlock and join the thumb and ring finger of your left hand into a circle with your right hand. Your right thumb should be on top of your left thumb. Extend the index, middle and small fingers of both hands so they touch each other at the finger tips.

Air: Join the thumb and the small (fourth) finger of your right hand into a circle. Interlock and join the thumb and small finger of your left hand into a circle with you right hand (you may find this position a bit difficult to start with but with practice it is manageable). Your right thumb should be on top of your left thumb. Extend the index, middle and ring fingers of both hands so they touch each other at the finger tips.

Spirit: Extend and join the thumb and four fingers of both hands and press them together in front of you so they are one, completing the elemental cycle.

Once mastered, this progression flows easily from one element to the next for meditation purposes and enables one to quickly bring the attributes of each element into focus for magical work by linking a physical action with the metaphysical connection.

In performing magical ritual, the more senses that can be engaged make creating and maintaining the visualization easier. Common approaches to this include:

Element	Sense	Aid
Earth	Touch	Sand / Rock / Crystal
Water	Taste	Water / Tea / Mead
Fire	Sight	Candle / Campfire
Air	Smell	Incense / Perfume
Spirit	Hearing	Chant / Chime

Similarly, connecting each element with a physical item gives one something to focus on when creating the visualization (more on this in the next chapter on Magical Ritual). Although it would be better to actually employ the sense memory of the element, using a physical representation is easier to use for communication when working with others, as the sense memory they use will likely be different from yours.

The symbols used below are commonly accepted and are based in the symbology of the Western Alchemy tradition. The mnemonics given are examples of things you might use to fix the symbol into your memory. Feel free to come up with your own.

Element	Symbol	Mnemonic
Earth		Rock over a molten iron core
Water		Paper cup
Fire		Flame over fuel (a candle)
Air		An updraft next to a mountain
Spirit		A focal point/ confluence

A traditional symbol used in magic is the pentagram. One of its uses is to symbolize the human body. Each element is associated with a point on the pentagram. The commonly accepted associations are:

I use a different set of associations, as I've found they allow me to better use the elements for a variety of reasons. Please use the approach with which you feel most comfortable.

My interpretation is:

A mnemonic you could use with my interpretation might be:

"I stand on Earth (matter) and Water (matter) holding Fire (energy) in my right hand and Air (energy) in my left hand."

As a note: traditionally the right side of the body is considered projective and the left side receptive. Earth and Fire are considered projective, Water and Air receptive. One of the reasons I prefer these associations is matter / energy and projective / receptive can be associated with bodily hemispheres of bottom / top and right side / left side.

The elements are also associated with the cardinal directions:

Element	Direction
Earth	North
Water	West
Fire	South
Air	East

There is much discussion about how this order came to be and if it's the only proper order. My theory is western traditions basically came from Britain and other Western European countries. So, the biggest body of water (the Atlantic Ocean) would have been in the West and the Sun would have been in the South. Earth seems the opposite of Fire so maybe it should go in the North, leaving Air to go in the East for lack of anywhere else to go.

The point is that: some magical traditions may not have complex and arcane origins. Sometimes they're simply based in the expediency of the moment.

Similarly, most people are right handed and so tend to take right hand paths when walking. With magical tradition Invocation is done moving in a clockwise direction (Deosil) and Banishing is done moving in a counter clockwise direction (Widdershins). It has become traditional, but if you're left handed or live in the Southern Hemisphere maybe reversing the directions would be more comfortable. If you do, as discussed in the Magical Ritual chapter, make sure you let folks know before you begin ritual so they won't run into each other.

To Learn the Elements:

Most magical application tries to affect our physical world. To do that one should understand how physical changes occur.

For example, to manifest in this world requires energy. When energy is collected it pulls energy out of the surrounding area. When energy levels fall, temperature falls also. Thus, if a ghost appears (manifests) then the surrounding air will grow colder.

Much can be learned of the elements, how they can be combined and how they interact, by studying the weather. All weather is caused by the Earth balancing differentials in heat (Fire) generated from the sun and from the interior of the Earth. By studying how energy flows in our universe, we can get a grounding in how energy flows in similar universes.

Rain / Snow (Water) is caused by evaporation (Fire) and moves because of wind (Air). Wind is created due to the temperature differentials between the water and the land (Earth) and between different locations within the water and land. Life (Earth) is sustained by rain / snow / clouds (Water) moved by the interplay of Air and Fire.

All things are connected. A butterfly's wings beating in China can ultimately create a hurricane in the Caribbean. However the physical creation of these flows may not happen quite as one would first expect.

To illustrate, to make things cooler first requires making them locally hotter. Hot air rises leaving a vacuum, drawing cooler air in from the surrounding area causing temperatures to fall. The bigger the differential between the hot spot and the surrounding area, the faster and harder the wind blows.

Similarly, to cause lightening to strike requires calling negative energy to one's self, creating a positive 'target'. Lightening (negative electrical energy) then strikes the positive target bringing things back into balance.

 ## *Practice One*

Go to a semi darkened room and light a candle. The room should be dark enough so you can distinguish the fine differences in the colors of the candle's flame.

Try to will the candle's flame to change color, sometimes creating more yellow and sometimes more blue. From an elemental magic approach this is done by adding / subtracting AIR not Fire. The more air one adds, the brighter and bluer the flame will burn, the less air the more yellow to orange.

∗∗∗

Returning to the first chapter for a moment, we learned the universe is made up of energy and all we experience are expressions of that energy. The same can be shown with the elements. Defining the universe in terms of elements gives us a conceptual framework that is intuitive to humans and easy to use, but, in truth, we are still dealing with energy.

When Earth becomes hot enough, it flows like water. When Water cools down enough, it becomes as solid as Earth, and when hot enough it becomes a gas like Air. When Air cools down enough it becomes a liquid. All is energy. All is vibration.

Practice Two

Usually people find they identify with / have an affinity for one element more than the others. Sometimes there will even be a hierarchy from best attuned to least attuned. It's important you find how you relate to the elements.

Even though you should experiment with all the elements and develop an understanding of them and their attributes, begin with the element you find most comfortable.

As examples, some people love the water and spend much of their free time doing things involving water. Others enjoy the air and love nothing better than to break free and fly. From there involve yourself with each element; immerse yourself in its nature.

It's also important you find your basic 'tone'. In the meditation practices we learned about sounding OM. Find a piano, or other instrument, sound a comfortable OM and find the note you're sounding on the instrument. This is probably close to your base tone. (If you lack access to an instrument, you can download an app to your smartphone that will tell you which tone you are sounding into the microphone. This is also helpful for those that have a 'tin ear' and find it difficult to hear the differences in tones.)

Once you find the note, experiment with its major, minor and octave chording. If it feels natural and easy to use to you, then it can be used as your base tone for magical ritual purposes. A check on this work is to find the musical key in which you most comfortably sing. If this is how you sing in the shower then you're probably right on key.

Magical Ritual

Most people use ritual to express magic. A ritual is simply a repeated set of actions done to achieve a result. It need not be complex. Drawing a circle around yourself isn't complicated and yet is one of the most fundamental and powerful rituals in magic. In contrast some rituals are very elaborate (e.g. a High Mass). Similarly, some rituals take a lot of preparation, while others are more spur-of-the-moment.

Rituals can vary greatly from individual to individual, from one group to another, even when they are supposed to achieve the same result. Why is this so? And how do we reconcile these differences to bring people together?

Variations in basal vibration rates (and thus harmonics) explain individual differences in magical practices / magical experiences and carry over into that person's ritual. A major task for the group is to coordinate, harmonize and focus each participant's vibration into a whole, to weave a magical tapestry from the individual threads. Thus, the focus should not be on the individual's basal vibration rate as much as on what must be done at the margin to bring it into harmony with the desired rate. This margin is highly variable because the starting place (the individual's basal rate) is highly variable.

For example, Solitaries can be more powerful than groups because they don't have to synchronize vibration rates. Old groups tend to be more powerful than young ones because people of like harmonics tend to stay while dis-harmonics tend to leave, resulting in a more correct vibratory fit and an easier harmonization / focus of the group's energies.

Ritual provides the means for most practitioners to:

- Build and focus energy
- Build and maintain a visualization
- Trigger sense memories and, over time, increase the power of the ritual
- Include others in magical work
- Increase their enjoyment in doing magic

The steps taken in doing individual ritual can be more free form and spontaneous. Group ritual works better with a more formal framework, which participants can discuss and agree upon beforehand. In either case some steps must be taken to make the ritual effective.

The first, surprisingly enough, is to define the objective of the ritual. Effective ritual requires a purpose that is clear, concise and limited in scope. Many rituals fail because their objectives are too vague or they try to accomplish too much. Magic can easily go awry if the intent isn't clear.

To illustrate, suppose you cast a spell to "find money". Don't complain if the result is you find a quarter in the street or you get an advertisement in the mail from a credit company offering to lend you money. Technically the spell worked. It just wasn't very helpful.

Objectives also should be reasonable, given the level of people involved and the intention. Many times rituals fail because they set outrageous / unlikely goals.

For example, a spell to 'win the lottery' is unlikely to manifest for the vast majority of people (and usually isn't something very important to those who can manifest it).

A better goal might be: to find a job paying $15 per hour within the next 30 days. Of course, to help the magic along, you then need to go apply for jobs that pay at least $15 per hour, and for which you have already developed the appropriate skills.

Similarly, it's difficult, at best, to generate and maintain focus to achieve one goal. It's almost impossible to do with ten. If multiple goals are identified then it's usually better to have multiple rituals sequentially than try to cram everything into one ritual.

Once the objective is defined, some like to do a 'reality check' by conducting a small ritual to see if the objective is appropriate or auspicious. If the results are negative then they don't move forward until the results become positive. This saves time and effort, especially in major undertakings, if the result is doomed to failure from the beginning. Others feel the whole point of magic is to manifest one's will and once the objective is defined then the magician should 'make it so'. Perhaps the truth is somewhere in *moon* the middle and depends upon the objective and the situation at the time. *astrol*

As we'll explore more deeply in the next chapter, designing magical ritual *etc.* is dependent upon several factors, including:

- Objective
- Participants
- Magical Abilities
- Magical Difficulty
- Powers / Entities Called
- Complexity

Each of these impacts how a ritual is designed, what steps are included, in what degree and with what level of duration and effort. The following focuses on group ritual. However, most of it can be easily adapted to individual ritual as well. Depending upon the type of ritual, some of the steps may be unneeded, can be done in a cursory manner or left out entirely. What to use, when and in what detail is part of the 'art' of magic.

The focus / objective of the ritual should determine what abilities / powers will be needed. Then active participants in the ritual are chosen based upon this list of abilities. Powerful manifestation is somewhat akin to cooking a good stew. It needs a solid base and the right mix of ingredients, blended together for just the right amount of time, to create something greater than the sum of its parts.

Active participants bring specific abilities to the ritual necessary to achieve the ritual's objective. Other participants should be included, perhaps, to lend support and/or provide a protected environment for those engrossed in manifesting the spell. Although sometimes disagreeable, it's important not to include those that will hamper or distract from the visualization / manifestation for whatever reasons. This is not to detract from them. It's simply their particular abilities may not be needed to achieve the objective, much like a good plumber is essential to making a well-crafted house but is not needed in the roofing of it.

Next, the tools / receptacles / costuming, and so forth, should be selected. For example, if sand will be used to represent Earth then in what will it be contained? How and when will it be placed there? Perhaps it would be better to use one or more crystals. In which case which ones? Why those instead of others? The same questions might apply to the use of incense to represent Air. Each of these should be identified and agreed upon by the participants beforehand. These accoutrements are powerful aids in creating and maintaining the visualization and should be chosen with regards to how well they resonate with the participants.

Next a common symbology to be used during the ritual should be selected. Within elemental magic, and many other traditions, this symbology begins with the circle.

The circle represents unity (the one), the oneness of all things within the circle. At the same time it creates polarity (the two) because it separates that which is inside the circle from that which is outside it. This allows for the sanctification of the workspace; provides a barrier against that which would disrupt the ritual or harm the participants and creates a place that is outside time and space (i.e. magical).

It's critical to note that although we speak of 'the circle' in fact physically it is three dimensional, more in the shape of an egg or ellipsoid. This manifests the trinity (the three): above, center and below; body, mind, spirit; and so on.

The four elements are placed at the four cardinal points. Adding spirit at the center gives us the five. Remembering we operate in three dimensions, including above and below gives us the Chakras (the seven).

Adding the ordinal points to the cardinal points and the center we can represent the Nine Worlds (the nine). And, by adding above and below again, we have the Tree of Life (the eleven) and can represent both the physical and metaphysical cosmologies with this symbology, bringing us full circle back to unity (the one).

Which things need to be represented, and in what detail, should be agreed upon before the ritual so they can be visualized appropriately, in context with the ritual.

We've answered why, who and, preliminarily, how. We need to answer the more logistical questions of where and when.

A location to perform the ritual must be selected. This selection includes all of the mundane considerations like: access, travel to and from, appropriateness, magical qualities, and the like. What time will the ritual occur from both magical (e.g. waxing moon, magical event) and mundane (e.g. time of day / night) aspects? How much space will be needed for the ritual to be carried out by the participants comfortably? If the ritual is large, does it need to be held in a place with good natural acoustics so that participants can hear what's going on (I have a natural aversion to using microphones and speakers in ritual.)? If the ritual will be long, where will people sit / lie down to rest? If done sky clad (nude) will appropriate privacy be available? How will mosquitos be dealt with? What protection(s), magical and mundane, will be necessary to deal with interruptions, the curious or the disruptive? The amount of effort and preplanning in this step is driven from the answers to the kind of questions above.

We now know enough, in general, to be able to design the ritual in detail. In doing so we move more into the metaphysical aspects of the ritual. The following assumes a fairly intricate ritual with several participants. Solitary ritual tends to be a bit more direct but still may include many or all of the following, depending on the magical objective.

If done as a group, the participants should first agree upon circle 'etiquette'. The etiquette should be based in helping create and maintain the group's visualization. For example, an incredibly disruptive act is for participants to simply walk out of a ritual, breaking the circle, because they forgot something or need to answer the call of nature. Establishing a way to correctly open and close the circle beforehand AND informing people they should use that process, if necessary, goes quite a ways in removing the disruptive effect.

Similarly, informing participants beforehand if gods / goddesses / entities / powers are going to be evoked or invoked during the ritual, and for what purpose, is not only simple courtesy but also can be critically important if one of the participants has a history with that particular entity or doesn't want to participate in such an evocation / invocation.

The necessity for, and the minimum amount of, magical preparation and purification that should be done before attending the ritual should be determined. At least participants should do something to ensure they don't bring negative energies to the ritual. A common approach is simply to bathe, both physically and psychically, before coming to ritual. This helps ensure one doesn't bring untoward conditions to the work.

Additionally, participants should at least ground themselves (i.e. stabilize their vibratory rate) so they don't bring a lot of extraneous, and potentially disharmonious, vibrations to the workplace. This will facilitate the individuals' centering and the group's harmonizing within the ritual.

Once the group has gathered and preliminaries have been observed, everyone should center themselves (bring their vibratory rate to their basal rate). Harmonizing is the act of synchronizing one's vibration with those others involved in the work and is much easier to do if everyone begins from familiar starting points.

There's discussion around whether this should be done before the formal beginning of the ritual or after. Within the vibratory model, at least a trial run should be done before because if this step can't be accomplished then the probability of successfully completing the ritual is low. The trial run doesn't have to be elaborate. One of the main functions of the leader of the ritual is to bring each participant into magical harmony with the other participants. The leader should take a moment to get a sense of each person's vibrations and then determine how harmony will be achieved during the ritual. If this can't be done then the ritual should either be refocused so the disharmony doesn't matter or the ritual should not be done at all.

The next step is to formally open the ritual. Opening is done by casting and then consecrating the circle. The opening begins the visualization and the common experience that will translate the subjective into the objective reality. It should not be done hurriedly, shoddily or insubstantially. It is the foundation for all that follows.

The amount of physical aids necessary for a complete and consistent metaphysical visualization is based upon the magical prowess of the participants. For example, casting the circle normally requires a physical demarcation be made. This can be a line drawn in the earth, a chalk mark made upon the floor or some other action to define the physical boundary.

Consecration, the closing of the circle, is the ritual act of creating the magical workspace. The space within the circle becomes a crossroads that exists outside space-time and is a receptacle of magical forces. Upon consecration, the participants should envision a magical and impenetrable barrier between the inside and the outside, an egg that physically exists in five dimensions (length, width, height, time and spirit) and that metaphysically can be connected to the eleven.

When the workspace has been created then it needs to be connected to the agreed upon metaphysical points, and appropriate markers should be placed to enable participants to visualize those connections. The connections to be made are based upon the work to be performed. The work informs the ritual not the other way around. Sometimes it's not necessary to call all the quarters, all the gods or all the elements to accomplish the goal. One should limit connections to those that are necessary. (That is, gods should not be summoned to simply hang around with nothing to do. It tends to sour one's relationship with them.)

Returning to our elemental example, a common approach to calling the quarters is to draw a pentagram at each station. To summon an element, one draws the pentagram starting at that element's point and moving deosil until the pentagram is completed.

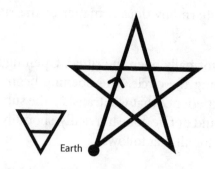

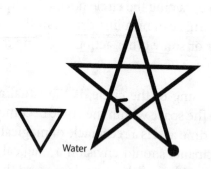

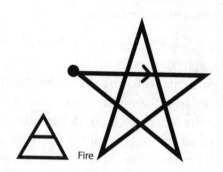

To banish an element, one draws the pentagram starting at that element's point and moving widdershins until the pentagram is completed.

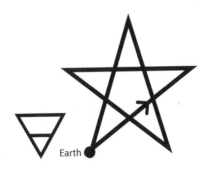

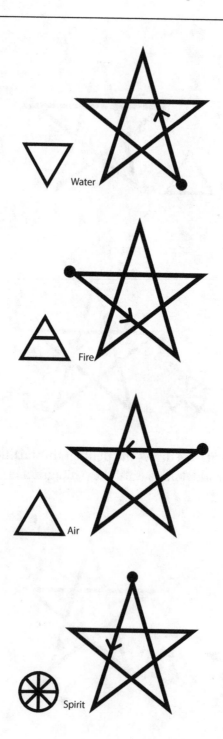

A similar approach is used when powers are personified (Gods, Goddesses and other entities (e.g. Dwarves, Elves, Fairies, Elementals)). The pentagram represents / empowers the person(s) doing the calling.

Although the terms invite, evoke and invoke are sometimes used interchangeably, it's critical to note the differences in the ways entities can be summoned.

To 'Invite' is to request an entity / power attend or add power to the ritual. Whether the entity responds to the entreaty or not is left to the entity.

In contrast, to 'Evoke' is more compelling and is more of a demand than a request. It causes the entity / power to manifest OUTSIDE the requestor. How the entity / power reacts to this demand tends to depend upon the entity, circumstances, purpose of the summoning, and so on.

To 'Invoke' is to compel the entity / power to manifest INSIDE the requestor. Although this allows the practitioner to more directly interface with and use the entity's powers, it can also be quite dangerous. The practitioner has, of his/her own free will, lowered his/her defenses to control the entity's intentions and substantially compromises his/her ability to banish the entity when desired.

When dealing with entities, usually Invocation is more dangerous / risky than Evocation, which in turn is more dangerous / risky than Invitation. One should review and understand the risks carefully before proceeding.

When calling, one should have a receptacle or representation the entity can manifest inside. This helps in the group's visualization and is good manners. When called the group should be able to visualize some sensorial change that shows the power / entity has joined the circle and inhabited the representation. For example, sand might turn a deeper brown, the smell of incense become richer or figurine take on a glow of power.

In doing magical work the called should be placed at points around the circle. The center of the circle is reserved for the representation of Man and is the focal point of the gathered power.

If something is to be worshipped ritual takes on a very different intent and the worshipped then is placed in the center (usually represented by an altar) and everything is prepared so the worshipped becomes the physical and metaphysical focus of the ritual.

After the circle is closed, and all of the initial participants, entities and powers have been gathered, then it is time to begin the work.

The first task in performing the work is to gather together, synchronize and merge the powers of the group, blending them into a focused harmony of vibrational energy.

A metaphor for this is how a laser in generated. Light is made up of a variety of frequencies going in all directions at once. A laser is generated by selecting only one frequency, getting those specific vibrations moving in the same direction in a coherent stream, then increasing their power and, finally, allowing them to be released, creating the laser beam.

Similarly, ritual harmonizing everyone's vibrations allows magical energy to be merged into a coherent stream. That energy, through the mechanisms of the ritual, is then amplified by augmenting the wave as it reaches its crests, much like a child goes higher and higher on a swing. Once the needed power is generated, it is then focused by the participants by visualizing on the magical intent of the work. Finally it is released into the world all at once to accomplish that work. Specifically how this is done varies from task to task and from group to group and is beyond the scope of this primer. However, an example ritual is discussed in the next chapter to give the reader a starting point.

Once the work is completed, the ritual can be closed and the circle opened. The steps done before the work are reversed. Entities are released (and thanked). Participants are again grounded so that returning to the mundane world is eased. The circle is ritually opened (de-consecrated) and the ritual equipment is disassembled / cleared up. Participants are then free to socialize or leave, as the magical work is complete.

Specifically with regards to elemental magic, it should be noted the elements are always with us. Thus 'calling' an element is not as much asking them to come from somewhere else as getting their attention. We prepare a place for them to reside and explicitly ask them to join us because we have created a circle that has a threshold to cross and we must 'invite them in' to the circle.

Creating and Performing Ritual

Many people learn by doing. Theory is fine but is sometimes difficult to apply. In this chapter we will work through a ritual from beginning to end. The focus is to show the thinking and methodology that goes into preparing a ritual rather than give you something to perform. This is a culmination and application of what this book is about.

The objective of this ritual is to create a defensive spell to remove a physical place from magical sight, to make it invisible. To achieve our objective we must first understand how invisibility is created. What, exactly, must be done to make something invisible?

Sight needs light (Fire). Physically sight of an object occurs due to reflection of certain wave lengths of light back to the observer. Perception of an object occurs when the mind processes that reflected light. Thus, there are several ways to stay hidden from sight.

Most defensive approaches offer a simple mirror spell to keep out unwanted eyes (e.g. Mirror, mirror, mirror so bright; Whether by day or by night; Reflect from here all others' sight; Mirror, mirror, mirror so bright.).

Although mirror spells may be effective, they lack subtlety and can set in motion a contest of wills to see whether the mirror can be broken. A better concept for this type of defensive magic is to develop a layered defense that gets progressively stronger / more direct as an attack is prosecuted. Each layer is based in using only the amount of force necessary to deter the attack. Operationally invisibility can be created in four ways:

Invisibility: The two physical ways to achieve invisibility are to let light pass through (i.e. transparency) so that no reflection occurs or to let light pass around (i.e. wave form) and re-form on the other side. That is, allow what is behind the object to appear on the face so the object doesn't differentiate from the background.

Obscurity: This refers to providing an indistinct image that is difficult to recognize. This can be done by a physical fog or through the perception by 'clouding the mind'.

Camouflage: This refers to changing the appearance of the object so that it blends into the surrounding landscape / environment. The object then does not stand out from the background and, thus, is not perceived by the viewer. To some extent this is a method to 'hide in plain sight'.

Reflection: This refers to reflecting the foreground back to the observer so the observer cannot see in. While hiding what's behind the mirror, it has the drawback of letting the observer know that something is there, hiding. Not allowing any reflection (the black hole approach) shares the same drawback.

Our ritual will be conducted inside a room that has an irregular shape because of furniture and the like. It would be nicer to have a bare room, but it probably wouldn't be practical to remove everything, do the ritual, and then put everything back. (This is one reason to develop a set of magical tasks one does before constructing or moving into a place. It's so much easier to do things before the place becomes cluttered with stuff.)

The location should be prepared by cleaning it (both physically and magically) to remove any existing contaminants. The amount of effort expended and level of detail depends upon the location. One would spend less time on a new dwelling than on an older one that had a history of magical / psychic issues.

Similarly, appropriate accouterments and accommodations should be gathered together before the ritual (see below). These items may / should also be cleaned, physically and magically, as deemed appropriate.

The space should be mapped out, physically and magically, dependent upon the ritual. Attention should be paid to the actions that will be done and how they will be done so the space and its contents don't present obstacles for the ritual. Grounding the space may also be necessary.

The participants should be selected based upon the work to be done. They should go through whatever preparation / purification necessary to be a viable member of the ritual. Grounding is normally part of this activity and should occur BEFORE the participant comes to the location so as to not disrupt other participants' groundings. Each participant should come to ritual with as consistent and pure a vibration as possible.

Circle etiquette should be communicated / agreed upon BEFORE the ritual. This is a critical step because most people have enough to deal with creating / maintaining a visualization. As the practice of ritual is to create a shared experience, those behaviors that distract from the shared experience can cause the ritual to fail.

The ritual should be explained to the participants BEFORE doing the ritual, so that participants know what to expect and their parts within the ritual. This should be done giving the participants sufficient time to prepare and learn their 'parts'. Participants should do whatever is necessary to learn their parts and the ritual. Good ritual is like good theater in that people should come knowing their lines, stage directions, tasks and responsibilities.   *use notes?*

Decide what symbology to use and what magical tasks will be performed within that symbology. For example, as the location is irregular, creating and closing the circle will be difficult. For this ritual the circle should include the walls of the structure. If it doesn't then the invisibility spell will only apply to the stuff inside the walls, leaving the structure still visible. This issue may be addressed by using incense smoke to create the circle at the walls rather than drawing a line on the floor.

Reach agreement with participants on operational details which may differ between groups or individuals. As examples, will creation / summoning be done deosil and dissolution / banishment be done widdershin? If symbols / tools will be used during the ritual, what do they represent and in what order should they be used? As the circle will at some point have to be opened / broken, will breaking the circle at a point be enough or will the entire circle have to be removed?

Established groups involving the same participants usually have this all worked out as part of their tradition. It's still a good idea to have the discussion so new initiates don't have to pick up the information by osmosis (consider it a part of their training) and older hands are reminded how the group conducts ritual, even if they do ritual differently as a Solitaire.

It's easy to forget things that will be needed during a ritual. Rummaging about for matches to light a candle usually will detract from the overall ambience of the ritual. So, it's helpful to make a list of what will be needed and check things off as they go into the box. Additionally this creates the opportunity to walk through the ritual in your mind and establish what will be done, in what order and with what tools.

For this ritual we will assume there are several novices that will need aids to help understand and visualize events within the ritual. The aids presented below are suggestions and may seem unnecessary to some. The ritual should be prepared based upon the work and the abilities of the participants. Results are dependent upon the common experience. It's usually better to help people accomplish their tasks than to simply expect them to do what's necessary even though they may struggle to do so.

Because of the location's constraints, incense will be used to create the circle. Stick incense creates smoke that can be wafted towards the walls so the circle will include the physical structure by going behind or around furniture, etc. A feather can be used to move the smoke where needed.

Frankincense is well known for its protective power and its ability to inhibit / drive out negative and unwanted influences. It seems a good choice for our concealment spell. Its smell and power will tend to permeate the walls continuing its protection after the ritual has been completed and giving a sensorial reminder that its protection is in place. When it can no longer be smelled, then perhaps the spell should be renewed.

The ritual, based in the elemental form of magic, will evoke all of the elements, including spirit. Representations and receptacles for each element will be needed. A bag of sand will be used for Earth and be contained in a small iron cauldron. A bottle of water will be used for Water and be contained in a chalice (cup). A candle will be used for Fire and be lit with a wooden match. An essential oil (Frankincense) will be used for Air and be contained in a diffuser with candle. As this incense will be used throughout the ritual, diffused incense is usually a better choice as compared to stick incense because it doesn't generate as much smoke that can irritate some while still is in keeping with the idea of protection mentioned above. A different incense might be used but, if so, should be selected so as to not negate the properties of the original incense. Spirit (Man) will be represented by the pentagram and will be drawn in the air and on the table using white sand (see below).

To help participants visualize events, engage their senses and focus energies several aids will be used. A table will be placed in the center of the circle. As each element has a color (Earth Green, Water Blue, Fire Orange and Air Yellow) brightly colored tape will be placed on the floor from each element's receptacle to the table representing the flow of that element's energies into the common pool. On the table, each element's contribution will be represented by its colored symbol drawn in its position at a point of a pentagram. This will be done using colored sand from sand pencils.

To further engage the senses, a chime will be selected for each element and sounded when that element is engaged in the work. To help participants remember the ritual experience, they will be given a magical tool for future use and aid them in their focus, reminding them of the ritual and adding to their magical tool boxes. So, each participant will receive a small piece of Malachite and of Tiger Eye.

In keeping with the objective, Malachite is a receptive stone known for its protective power and ability to detect and guard against danger. Its banded layers can be used to disguise one's intent and act as a cloak of invisibility against intruders. Traditionally, the left hand is the receptive hand, so participants will hold this stone in their left hands.

Tiger Eye is projective, known for its protective power and its ability to increase one's strength, power and courage. Traditionally, the right hand is the projective hand, so participants will hold this stone in their right hands. Using these aids helps filter each participant's energies, helping to synchronize them and make them more coherent.

This gives us the following supplies list for our ritual:

Supplies

1	small bag each colored sand (Green, Blue, Orange, Yellow and White)
5	sand pens / tubes (filled with the colored sand)
1	small bag regular brown sand
1	small cauldron
1	glass bottle, or small pitcher, of water
1	medium chalice
1	medium white candle
1	box of wooden matches
1	essential oil diffuser
1	small, white, unscented 'tea' candle
1	bottle of Frankincense essential oil
2	Frankincense incense sticks
1	medium sized feather
1	small Malachite stone for each participant
1	small Tiger's Eye stone for each participant
5	chimes in one key (e.g. A, D, F#, Octave A & D)
4	rolls of colored Duct tape (Green, Blue, Orange, and Yellow)
1	table
	Enough chairs for everyone to have a seat
	(and a compass if you don't know where North is.)

The table should be placed in the center of the work area. The feather, incense sticks, sand pens and the box of matches should be placed on the table for use in the ritual. The cauldron and bag of regular brown sand are placed in the north, the water bottle and chalice in the west, the white candle in the south and the oil diffuser, tea candle and bottle of essential oil in the east.

The appropriately colored duct tape should be placed on the floor from each of the cardinal points at the edge of the circle to the table in the center. These symbolize the conduit of power from the element to the central point of the circle.

Each person, except for the leader, is given a Malachite and Tiger's Eye stone when the group gathers together to begin the ritual. As novices will be participating, the leader or a mentor should explain to them how to use the stones magically before the ritual.

The chairs should be placed out of the way (but still inside the circle). Once the circle has been closed and the elements evoked, the chairs can be brought out for the main portion of the work. When the work is done, they can again be placed out of the way (but still inside the circle) for the releasing of the elements and opening of the circle.

Moving chairs around creates some logistical issues, and a significantly bigger circle. On the other hand, it may be asking too much of the participants to stand on their feet for the 2-3 hours it takes to perform this ritual. Being able to sit down is usually appreciated.

Evoking the elements:

For the ritual evoking each element will require three actions: First, at each station the appropriate pentagram is drawn in the air and an evocation is spoken to call the element. The element's receptacle is filled with its representation (e.g. water is poured into the chalice) and the agreed upon chime is sounded to show the element's arrival into the circle and to help participants pair the chime's vibration with the element.

The drawing of the pentagram (man) symbolizes the group's drawing the power of each element into the ritual. Each drawing is specific to the element being called.

The receptacles are placed at the cardinal points (Earth/north, Air/east, Fire/south, Water/west) at the edge of the circle so that each element can act as protector and its power flows into the circle. This also provides a distance between mutually antagonistic elements (e.g. Fire and Water).

Each element's power is drawn to the center table where they attach to, and are harmonized inside of, the pentagram drawn on the table. Drawn by man and controlled by his/her spirit (symbolized at the top of the pentagram). This approach creates the five (the four cardinal points and the center) in accordance with elemental magic.

Performing Magic:

Performing magic is done in four steps:

- Gathering energy
- Focusing energy
- Manifesting energy
- Releasing energy

Within this ritual, each element is paired with a particular chime. Sounding the element's paired chime helps the participants gather its energy, and synchronize / harmonize their vibrations to the needed one, bringing the magical energy into coherency.

Focusing the energy to the magical intent will be done using specific images and guided meditation allowing each participant to visualize what the energy should do.

Manifesting the energy will be done also through guided meditation by specifically bridging the magical intent from the metaphysical to the physical world.

Releasing the energy occurs last within the guided meditation and includes the strong visualization of the energy impacting our physical reality. This follow through is important and frequently forgotten. Participants must perceive an impact caused by their actions to help solidify the ritual's effects.

Calling people to ritual:

Letting participants know about a ritual can be done in a variety of ways. The amount of detail / instruction provided is dependent upon the level of the participants. Given the several novices expected to join this ritual the following memo / email might be used:

Upcoming Ritual

Location:

Date / Time:

Preparation / Purification:
Please bathe / shower before coming. You might use this as an opportunity to 'wash your cares away'. If you have any other particular preparation / purification rituals, please feel free to do them. The point is to put aside the pressures of the day before coming to ritual. We'll be using a small amount of incense, so please don't use any strong perfumes.

Grounding / Centering:
Grounding is achieving a stable vibrational level. Centering is bringing that level to your basal rate. Grounding is very hard to do if your mind is fragmented by the day's worries. As with the above, the point is to clear your mind, calm yourself and get in a positive frame of mind to join in ritual. If you're unsure how to center, don't be too concerned. We'll do some centering as part of the ritual.

Clothing:
As this will be a working session, ceremonial clothing isn't necessary. Please wear whatever you'll be comfortable in for three hours. We suggest you stay with natural fibers (e.g. cotton, wool) as much as possible, as man-made fabrics tend to be harder to work through when doing elemental magic. For example, socks and shoes tend to be nylon and synthetic rubber now-a-days. Although removing shoes is fine, socks may be another story.

Supplies:

Supplies will be provided. There will be bran muffins and fruit juice for enjoyment after ritual. If you have something you'd like to bring / share, please feel free to do so, but it isn't required. (No alcohol please.)

Circle Etiquette:

Magical ritual originated in a much slower, gentler time. Additionally, maintaining focus / concentration is critical to success. So, please leave your cell phones, etc., in your car. If you can't 'unplug' for the required time, please let this opportunity pass by.

Please come to ritual with, at least, no negative feelings and an open mind. Plan to actively take part. If you are uncomfortable joining in, please let this opportunity pass by, as it is a working session rather than a training session.

As this is an elemental ritual, there will be NO gods / goddesses invoked nor oaths taken during this ritual. There is one affirmation in the work that, simply put, says that we will endeavor to do good works. Anything you feel uncomfortable with, you can simply choose not to say.

See you soon.

***

Depending on the ritual and the group, if designated participants will have speaking parts then what they should say, and when, should be sent to them well in advance of the ritual so they can 'learn their lines'. For established rituals and experienced participants this may not be necessary unless a novice is expected to take part. Similarly if a call / response format is used (e.g. 'so mote it be') then it also probably isn't necessary as people will pick up the response quickly within the ritual itself.

The ritual site should be prepared appropriately well before the meeting time and all items to be used accounted for and in place. Participants should be courteous enough to arrive prepared and on time. Once ritual has begun, if possible, interruptions (e.g. people arriving late) should not be allowed.

The above is the logistical side of ritual that gets the right people to the right place at the right time with the right tools. The ritual itself is far more subjective than objective. Conducting ritual is more of an art. As a note: it takes most people time to create a good visualization, so give them time to do so. Try not to rush the ritual.

Performing the work

To help participants visualize for this ritual, everyone should go outside the room and look at it from each side to see what is there.

Before the main ritual, participants should center their vibrations and begin to harmonize them so they can act as a coherent force. One way to do this is through guided meditation and using a 2 beat breathing pattern. Participants should be in comfortable positions for this as discussed in Chapter 3 and have their eyes closed.

The leader says:

"We will begin centering with a 2 beat breathing: 2 beats inhale, 2 beats hold, 2 beats exhale, 2 beats hold and repeat.

Inhale
Hold
Exhale
Hold

(Repeat until everyone is in rhythm.)

Inhale the air.
Feel it fill your body.
Hold it.
Let it flow throughout your body.

Exhale the air.
Push it out, taking all impurities with it.
Hold onto the stillness for a moment.

(Repeat until everyone has found stillness.)

See the light.
Inhale the light.
See it fill your body.
Hold it.
Let it flow throughout your body.

Exhale the light.
Use the light to push out the shadows,
Leaving only light to remain.
See the light, inhale the light.

(Continue for a few cycles.)

Breathe normally.
Open your eyes.
Let us begin."

Main Ritual

Casting the Circle:

Starting at north, one person lights a stick of frankincense while another holds it.

Moving deosil, one person holds the incense while the other uses a feather to waft the smoke towards the wall.

The leader explains that the incense is being used to create a circle that will encompass the entire room including the walls. Participants should visualize this happening, seeing the smoke flowing around and behind furniture, up and down the walls, across the floor and ceiling, creating a solid bubble within which work can be done.

After the pair have completed a circuit of the room, the leader formally joins (closes) the circle by drawing a pentagram deosil starting at Spirit where the two ends of the circle meet. The leader then consecrates the circle with:

Consecration:

"The circle is closed.
Within it we are masters of our fate
Within it we come, magical works to create
Within it we stand outside time and space
And so we now consecrate this place
The circle is closed.
So mote it be."

All say:

"So mote it be."

Evoking the elements:
(Pentagram. Then receptacle. Lastly, chimes)

<u>Facing north at the edge of the circle.</u>

The leader draws a summoning pentagram in the air starting at Earth.

All say:

"We evoke Earth. Bring to our circle your strength and stability. We have prepared a place for you here."

The leader pours regular brown sand into the cauldron, sets the cauldron on the floor and places the bag out of the way for use later.

All say:

"Join us now."

The Earth chime is rung.

(Participants should visualize Earth's power suffusing the sand and its presence materializing.)

The leader moves deosil 1 ¾ circuits until facing west at the edge of the circle. When the leader passes the north in the circuit all others turn in place to follow the leader's journey (the ¾ circuit) until all face the west.

The leader draws a summoning pentagram in the air starting at Water.

All say:

"We evoke Water. Bring to our circle your flowing power and purifying spirit. We have prepared a place for you here."

The leader pours water from a pitcher into the chalice, sets the chalice on the floor and places the pitcher out of the way for use later.

All say:

"Join us now."

The Water chime is rung.

(Participants should visualize Water's power suffusing the chalice and its presence materializing.)

The leader moves deosil 1 ¾ circuits until facing south at the edge of the circle. When the leader passes the west in the circuit all others turn in place to follow the leader's journey (the ¾ circuit) until all face the south.

The leader draws a summoning pentagram in the air starting at Fire.

All say:

"We evoke Fire. Bring to our circle your energy and dynamic power. We have prepared a place for you here."

The leader lights the candle and sets the candle on the floor.

All say:

"Join us now."

The Fire chime is rung.

(Participants should visualize Fire's power suffusing the candle's flame and its presence materializing.)

The leader moves deosil 1 ¾ circuits until facing east at the edge of the circle. When the leader passes the south in the circuit all others turn in place to follow the leader's journey (the ¾ circuit) until all face the east.

The leader draws a summoning pentagram in the air starting at Air.

All say:

"We evoke Air. Bring to our circle your ability to connect and permeate our world. We have prepared a place for you here."

The leader places oil in the diffuser, lights the candle, places the candle in the diffuser, and sets the diffuser on the floor.

All say:

"Join us now."

The Air chime is rung.

(Participants should visualize Air's power suffusing the incense's smoke and its presence materializing.)

The leader moves deosil 1 ¾ circuits until facing north at the edge of the circle. When the leader passes the east in the circuit all others turn in place to follow the leader's journey (the ¾ circuit) until all face the north. The leader then moves to the bottom (southern edge) of the table and faces north. All others turn so they face the center.

The leader draws a pentagram in the air starting at Spirit.

All say:

"We invoke Spirit. Bring to our circle harmony and focus our wills to fulfill our intent. We have prepared a place for you here within the fellowship we hold in our hearts."

"Join us now."

The Spirit chime is rung.

(If the ritual is working, when the words are spoken and the chime rung participants should experience an uplifting feeling, a strengthening bond and an increased harmony with the others in the circle.)

All say:

"We welcome the five elements and invoke their powers to aid us in our work."

(Using the white sand pen, the leader draws a pentagram on the center of the table, deosil, starting at Spirit. Then, as each element's name is spoken, the symbol for that element is drawn at its place, deosil, next to the pentagram with the appropriately colored sand pen.)

"Earth"	(Green)
"Water"	(Blue)
"Fire"	(Orange)
"Air"	(Yellow)
"and Spirit"	(White)

(As each symbol is drawn participants should visualize each element's energies flowing from its receptacle to its symbol on the table, causing that symbol to glow with power.)

All five chimes are then rung in order so that they merge into and resonate as one sound. The group pauses a moment to harmonize themselves with the collective power of the elements and of the group.

(Chairs can now be placed for use facing the center of the circle. Participants remain standing.)

Creating Invisibility:

The leader stands in the center of the group.

The Fire and Water chimes are rung together.

The group meditates for a moment to gather and harmonize Fire and Water energy.

All face north.

The leader says,

"Light is created by Fire and flows like Water. The light moving outward from this room allows people outside to see it, but this can be changed by magic.

See the light from those things behind us flow around us, coming back together in front of us so we disappear and people can only see what is behind."

The group takes a moment to establish the visualization, moving the scene that is on the opposite side of the room to the targeted side, replacing it and removing it from view. When done,

The leader says:

"Fire's light that lights all space
Flow like Water around this place
Show what's behind to those who look
Let the face be forsook."

The group turns 90 degrees and repeats the ritual from the ringing of the Fire and Water chimes until each wall of the room has been magically addressed. Additionally, the group should address the floor and ceiling.

The group then sits, facing the center.

Creating Obscurity:

The Air and Water chimes are rung together.

The group meditates for a moment to gather and harmonize Air and Water energy.

The leader says.

"Fog is created by air and water. As fog obscures the world from physical sight, magic can be used to obscure the world from mystical sight.

See the fog enveloping the outside of this room starting just outside its walls. See the room become indistinct and fade from view. The fog continuing to thicken until the room can no longer be seen."

The group takes a moment to establish the visualization. When done,

The leader says:

"Air and Water make a haze
To shield this place from magical gaze
Changing sight within the mist
To show this place does not exist."

Creating Camouflage:

The Earth and Water chimes are rung together.

The group meditates for a moment to gather and harmonize Earth and Water energy.

All stand and face north.

The leader says:

"Buildings are created from Earth and Water. As water can make earth flow, magic can make its images flow. See the room on the left of us. Pull on its image, stretching it so it covers half of our room. See the room on the right of us. Pull on its image, stretching it so it covers half of our room. Make where they join seamless so they touch each other."

The group takes a moment to establish the visualization. When done,

The leader says:

"Earth and Water take the sight
Of what is on the left and right
Blend them together to meet as one
And hide this place when it is done."

The group turns 90 degrees and repeats the ritual from the ringing of the Earth and Water chimes until each wall of the room has been magically addressed. Additionally, the group should address the floor and ceiling.

The group then sits, facing the center.

Creating Reflection:

The Earth chime is rung.

The group meditates for a moment to gather Earth energy.

The leader says:

"Mirrors are made of glass and silver and come from the Earth. Magic can change the earth. See the outside of our room. See it change, becoming more and more reflective. See your face in the outside of our room. See the clothes you're wearing. See what's behind you."

The group takes a moment to establish the visualization. When done,

The leader says:

"Earth, make this place a shield of glass
Through which no mystical light may pass
With silver make a mirror so bright
To reflect from here all magical sight
Whether by day or by night
Until we choose to return to sight."

The leader says:

"Before finishing a good craftsman checks the work to make sure it is good and true, and so should we. Use your magical sight to see the outside of the room. Can you see yourself in its mirror?"

The group takes a moment to complete the task.

"Take a few steps back. Do the images of the rooms on our left and right meet seamlessly so they appear joined in the middle?"

The group takes a moment to complete the task.

"Take a few steps back. Do you lose our room in the fog? Does it gradually disappear from view?"

The group takes a moment to complete the task.

"Take a few steps back. Does the fog also disappear and you see what's around us but not us? Do you see only those things behind?"

The group takes a moment to complete the task.

"It is well done. So mote it be."

All reply: "So mote it be."

(Chairs should now be placed out of the way. Participants stand facing the center.)

Returning power to the elements:

(The leader stands at the south edge of the table facing north)

The leader says:

"Through the magic of the elements we have completed our work."

(As the leader says each element's name its chime is struck. The leader then smudges out that element's symbol on the table. As this occurs participants should visualize each element's power returning from the table to its receptacle.)

"Earth"   (Green)
"Water"   (Blue)
"Fire"   (Orange)
"Air"   (Yellow)

The leader moves from the table to the east point of the circle. All face east.

Releasing the Elements:

(Chimes. Then pentagram. Lastly, receptacle. As each element is released participants should visualize its power leaving its receptacle and the receptacle returning to its mundane state.)

The Air chime is rung.

All say:

"We thank Air for bringing connection and permeation to our circle."

The leader draws a banishing pentagram in the air starting at Air.

The leader says:

"Feel free to take your leave from our circle."

"Go in Peace."

The leader removes the candle from the diffuser, blows out the flame and then replaces the candle in the diffuser.

The leader moves widdershins 1 ¾ circuits until facing south at the edge of the circle. When the leader passes the east in the circuit all others turn in place to follow the leader's journey (the ¾ circuit) until all face the south.

The Fire chime is rung.

All say:

"We thank Fire for bringing energy and dynamic power to our circle."

The leader draws a banishing pentagram in the air starting at Fire.

The leader says:

"Feel free to take your leave from our circle."

"Go in Peace."

The Leader snuffs the candle out with his/her fingers.

The leader moves widdershins 1 ¾ circuits until facing west at the edge of the circle. When the leader passes the south in the circuit all others turn in place to follow the leader's journey (the ¾ circuit) until all face the west.

The Water chime is rung.

All say:

"We thank Water for bringing flowing power and purifying spirit to our circle."

The leader draws a banishing pentagram in the air starting at Water.

The leader says:

"Feel free to take your leave from our circle."

"Go in Peace."

The leader pours the water from the chalice into the pitcher and sets both down on the floor.

The leader moves widdershins 1 ¾ circuits until facing north at the edge of the circle. When the leader passes the west in the circuit all others turn in place to follow the leader's journey (the ¾ circuit) until all face the north.

The Earth chime is rung.

All say:

"We thank Earth for bringing strength and stability to our circle."

The leader draws a banishing pentagram in the air starting at Earth.

The leader says:

"Feel free to take your leave from our circle."

"Go in Peace."

The leader pours the sand from the cauldron into a bag and sets both on the floor.

<u>The leader turns and moves to the south edge of the table and faces north. All others face the center.</u>

All say:

"We maintain our spirits. May we continue to better them, bring light to the darkness, joy to the sorrowful and peace to the world."

The leader smudges out the Spirit symbol and then the pentagram on the table.

Closing

Grounding

The leader says:

"It is meet that we ground ourselves before we end our ritual. Please join me.

Inhale
Hold
Exhale
Hold

(Repeat until everyone is in rhythm.)

Inhale the air.
Feel it fill your body.
Hold it.
Let it flow throughout your body.

Exhale the air.
Push it out.
Hold onto the stillness for a moment.

(Repeat until everyone has found stillness. The count continues unspoken.)

Feel the vibration of the universe.
Feel its beat, slow and steady.
Feel your body respond.
Feel your heartbeat, slow and steady.
Feel your vibration, slow and steady.
Feel your spirit, slow and steady.

(Continue for a few cycles.)

Breathe normally and open your eyes."

Opening the circle:

The leader moves to the north at the edge of the circle. All face north.

The leader breaks the circle by 'cutting' it with his/her hand.

All should visualize the magical energies of the circle dissipating back into the universe.

The leader says:

"The circle is open.
We now return to the mundane world.
Rejoining those outside the circle.
We now de-consecrate this place, for our work is done.
The circle is open.
So mote it be."

All reply: "So mote it be."

All help:

Disassemble the space / location.
Clean up, replace, pack accouterments and accommodations.

And finally the time has come to have food, drink and company.

Final Thoughts

Hopefully the study and practice of the concepts in this book will help you develop as a magician and as a person. To bring us full circle, we began with the premise that the universe is inherently in balance and must maintain that balance by its very nature. As one's power grows, so does one's ability to move the universe out of balance. Thus, as one's power grows, one tends to use that power less and less.

Developing magical abilities may be easier than developing foresight, understanding, compassion and wisdom, but developing these character traits is probably of even more importance.

With foresight one can perceive events and their consequences early enough so that small changes (small uses of power) can have big impacts. To paraphrase Sun Tzu in *The Art of War*, the greatest general is the one who can win the war without fighting.

With understanding one can choose the path that creates the smallest ripples, soon returning to stillness. Perfection is a quiet thing, so smoothly done as not to seem worthy of notice and somehow creating the impression for others that 'things just magically worked out'.

With compassion one can learn not to judge too harshly nor too quickly. Hurtful consequences from someone's actions can be unintentional and not necessarily done with malice aforethought, but through ignorance, carelessness or an immaturity that precludes compassion and understanding. Humans are neither gods nor animals, but somewhere in between, and we are all fragile in one way or another. Foresight, understanding and compassion help one respond to events rather than simply react to them.

With wisdom one can balance one's actions by sometimes being what goes around and sometimes being what comes around and in so doing immerse one's self in the flow to become one with the universe.

I hope you all fare well.

Selected Readings

I have read many, many books over the years. For your consideration I've listed below some of the ones I've kept.

Andrews, Ted. Animal Speak, The Spiritual & Magical Powers of Creatures Great & Small. Llewellyn Publications, 1993.

Ashcroft-Nowicki, Delores and Brennan, J.H. Magical Use of Thought Forms: A Proven System of Mental & Spiritual Empowerment. Llewellyn Publications, 2002.

Aswynn, Freya. Northern Mysteries and Magick: Runes, Gods, and Feminine Powers. Llewellyn Publishing, 2006.

Bardon, Franz. Initiation into Hermetics. Ruggeberg-Verlag, 1993.

Buckland, Raymond. Buckland's Complete Book of Witchcraft. Llewellyn Publications, 2001.

—. Signs Symbols & Omens: An Illustrated Guide to Magical & Spiritual Symbolism. Llewellyn Publishing, 2003.

Burt, Christopher C and Stroud, Mark. Extreme Weather: A Guide & Record Book. W.W. Norton & Company Inc., 2007.

Butler, W.E. How to Read the Aura and Practice Psychometry, Telepathy, & Clairvoyance. Destiny Books, 1998.

Byock, Jesse. Viking Age Iceland. Penguin Books, 2001.

Cheung, Theresa. The Element Encyclopedia of the Psychic World. Harper Element, 2006.

Clover, Carol J and Lindow, John. Old Norse-Icelandic Literature: A Critical Guide. University of Toronto Press, 2005.

Colum, Padraic. Nordic Gods and Heroes. Dover Publications, 1996.

Conway, D.J. Magickal, Mystical Creatures. Llewellyn Publications, 2003.

Cox, John D. Weather for Dummies. Hungry Minds, 2000.

Crossley-Holland, Kevin. The Norse Myths. Pantheon Books, 1980.

Crowley, Aleister. 777 and Other Qabalistic Writings of Aleister Crowley. Weiser Books, 1986.

Cunningham, David Michael. Creating Magickal Entities: A Complete Guide to Entity Creation. Egregore Publishing, 2003.

Cunningham, Scott and Harrington, David. Spell Crafts: Creating Magical Objects. Llewellyn Publishing, 2007.

—. The Magical Household: Spells & Rituals for the Home. Llewellyn Publishing, 2007.

Cunningham, Scott. Cunningham's Encyclopedia of Crystal, Gem & Metal Magic. Llewellyn Publications, 1995.

—. Cunningham's Encyclopedia of Magical Herbs. Llewellyn Publications, 2001.

—. Earth Power Techniques of Natural Magick. Llewellyn Publications, 2004.

—. Earth, Air, Fire & Water: More Techniques of Natural Magic. Llewellyn Publications, 2003.

—. The Complete Book of Incense, Oils & Brews. Llewellyn Publishing, 1998.

Davidson, H.R. Ellis. Gods and Myths of Northern Europe. Penguin Books, 1964.

DeLaurence, L.W. The Lesser Key of Solomon Goetia: The Book of Evil Spirits. DeLaurence, Scott & Co., 1916.

Denning, Malita and Phillips, Osborne. Practical Guide to Psychic Powers: Awaken Your Sixth Sense. Llewellyn Publishing, 2008.

—. The Llewellyn Practical Guide to Astral Projection, the Out of Body Experience. Llewellyn Publications, 1994.

—. The Llewellyn Practical Guide to Psychic Self-defense & Well-being. Llewellyn Publishing, 1995.

Drew, A.J. A Wiccan Formulary and Herbal. Career Press, 2005.

Elliott, Ralph W.V. Runes: An Introduction. St. Martin's Press, 1989.

Fortune, Dion. Psychic Self-Defense: A Study in Occult Pathology and Criminality. The Aquarian Press, 1987.

Franklin, Anna. Working with Fairies: Magick, Spells, Potions, & Recipes to Attract & See Them. Career Press, 2006.

Gonzalez-Wippler, Migene. The Complete Book of Spells, Ceremonies & Magic. Llewellyn Publishing, 2004.

Gordon, Jonathan. Healing Sounds: The Power of Harmonics. Healing Arts Press, 2002.

Greer, John Michael. Encyclopedia of Natural Magic. Llewellyn Publications, 2005.

—. The Druid Magic Handbook: Ritual Magic Rooted in the Living Earth. Weiser Books, 2007.

—. The New Encyclopedia of the Occult. Llewellyn Publishing, 2004.

Grinder, John and Bandler, Richard. Trance-Formations: Neuro-Linguistic Programming and the Structure of Hypnosis. Real People Press, 1981.

Harner, Michael. The Way of the Shaman. Harper Collins Publishers, 1990.

Hartman, Franz. Magic: White and Black. Kessinger Publishing Company, 7th ed.

Haskins, Jim. Voodoo & Hoodoo. Original Publications, 1978.

Hollander, Lee M. The Poetic Edda. University of Texas Press, 1994.

Hopman, Ellen Evert. A Druid's Herbal for the Sacred Earth Year. Destiny Books, 1995.

Kraig, Donald Michael. Modern Magick: Eleven Lessons in the High Magickal Arts. Llewellyn Publications, 1994.

Kronzck, Allan Zola and Elizabeth. The Sorcerer's Companion: A Guide to the Magical World of Harry Potter. Broadway Books, 2001.

LaVoie, Nicole. Return to Harmony: Creating Harmony and Balance Through Frequencies of Sound. Sound Wave Energy Press, 1996.

Lawless, Julia. The Encyclopedia of Essential Oils: The Complete Guide to the Use of Aromatics in Aromatherapy, Herbalism, Health & Well-Being. Barnes & Nobles Books, 1995.

Leet, Leonora. The Secret Doctrine of the Kabbalah: Recovering the Key to Hebraic Sacred Science. Inner Tradition, 1999.

Leifur Eiriksson Publishing. The Sagas of Icelanders: A Selection. Penguin Books, 2001.

Liddell, Samuel and MacGregor, Mathers. The Goetia: The Lesser Key of Solomon the King. Weiser Books, 1997.

Lindow, John. Norse Mythology: A Guide to the Gods, Heroes, Rituals, and Beliefs. Oxford University Press, 2001.

Lipp, Deborah. The Elements of Ritual: Air, Fire, Water & Earth in the Wiccan Circle. Llewellyn Publishing, 2003.

Mack, Carol K and Dinah. A Field Guide to Demons, Fairies, Fallen Angels, and Other Subversive Spirits. Henry Holt and Company, 1998.

Mathers, S.L. MacGregor. The Greater Key of Solomon. Digiread.com Publishing, 2006.

McMoneagle, Joseph. Remote Viewing Secrets: A Handbook. Hampton Roads Publishing Company, 2000.

Miller, Jason. Protection & Reversal Magick: A Witch's Defense Manual. Career Press, 2006.

Miller, R Michael and Harper, Josephine M. The Psychic Energy Workbook: An Illustrated Course in Practical Psychic Skills. Sterling Publishing Co., Inc., 1990.

Miller, Richard Alan and Iona. The Magical and Ritual Use of Perfumes. Destiny Books, 1990.

Mountfort, Paul Rhys. Nordic Runes: Understanding, Casting, and Interpreting the Ancient Viking Oracle. Destiny Books, 2003.

Murchie, Guy. Music of the Spheres. The Riverside Press, 1961.

Neal, Carl F. Incense: Crafting & Use of Magickal Scents. Llewellyn Publications, 2004.

O'Donoghue, Heather. Old Norse-Icelandic Literature: A Short Introduction. Blackwell Publishing, 2004.

Olsen, Kaedrich. Runes for Transformation: Using Ancient Symbols to Change Your Life. Weiser Books, 2008.

OSHO International Foundation. OSHO Zen Tarot: The Transcendental Game of Zen. St. Martin's Press, 1994.

Ouseley, S.G.J. Colour Meditations with Guide to Colour Healing. L.N. Fowler & Co. LTD., 1986.

Paxson, Diana L. Essential Asatru: Walking the Path of Norse Paganism. Kensington Publishing Corp., 2006.

—. Taking Up the Runes: A Complete Guide to Using Runes in Spells, Rituals, Divination, and Magic. Weiser Books, 2005.

Penczak, Christopher. The Witch's Shield: Protection Magick & Psychic Self-Defense. Llewellyn Publishing, 2004.

Phillips, Osborne. Astral Projection Plain & Simple. Llewellyn Publications, 2003.

Rockport Publishers. Color Harmony Workbook. Rockport Publishers, 2001.

Rumstuckle, Cornelius. The Book of Wizardry: The Apprentice's Guide to the Secrets of the Wizard's Guild. Llewellyn Publishing, 2005.

Simmons, Robert and Ahsian, Naisha. The Book of Stones: Who They Are & What They Teach. Heaven & Earth Publishing, 2007.

Skinner, Stephen. The Complete Magician's Tables. Llewellyn Publishing, 2009.

Slate, Joe H. Aura Energy for Health Healing & Balance. Llewellyn Publications, 2004.

Sullivan, Tammy. Elemental Witch: Fire, Air, Water, Earth, Discover Your Natural Affinity. Llewellyn Publications, 2006.

Thorsson, Edred. Futhark: A Handbook of Rune Magic. Samuel Weiser, Inc., 1984.

—. Northern Magic: Mysteries of the Norse, Germans and English. Llewellyn Publishing, 1993.

—. Runelore: A Handbook of Esoteric Runology. Samuel Weiser, Inc., 1992.

—. The Nine Doors of Midgard: A Complete Curriculum of Rune Magic. Llewellyn Publishing, 1994.

Toro, Gianluca and Thomas, Benjamin. Drugs of the Dreaming: Oneirogens: Salvia Divinorum and Other Dream Enhancing Plants. Park Street Press, 2007.

Tyson, Donald. Three Books of Occult Philosophy Written by Henry Cornelius Agrippa of Nettesheim. Llewellyn Publishing, 2006.

Webster, Richard. Amulets & Talismans for Beginners, How to Choose, Make & Use Magical Objects. Llewellyn Publications, 2004.

Webster, Richard D. Aura Reading for Beginners. Llewellyn Publications, 2003.

Whitcomb, Bill. The Magician's Companion: A Practical & Encyclopedic Guide to Magical & Religious Symbolism. Llewellyn Publishing, 1994.

Wild, Leon D. The Runes Workbook: A Step-by-Step Guide to Learning the Wisdom of the Staves. Thunder Bay Press, 2004.

Yoder, Don and Graves, Thomas E. Hex Signs: Pennsylvania Dutch Barn Symbols & Their Meaning. Stackpole Books, 2000.

Young, Jean I. The Prose Edda of Snorri Sturluson: Tales from Norse Mythology. University of California Press, 1984.

Yronwode, Catherine. Hoodoo Herb and Root Magic. The Lucky Mojo Curio Co., 2002.

Zell-Ravenheart, Oberon and DeKirk, Ash. A Wizard's Bestiary. Career Press, 2007.

Zell-Ravenheart, Oberon and Morning Glory. Creating Circles & Ceremonies: Rituals for All Seasons and Reasons. Career Press, 2006.

Zell-Ravenheart, Oberon. Companion for the Apprentice Wizard. Career Press, 2006.

—. Grimoire for the Apprentice Wizard. Career Press, 2004.

Thank you for supporting independent publishing.

About the Author

J M Conley, a Solitaire wizard, has studied the occult since childhood. As a metaphysician he has always been more interested in the commonalities between the various paths than the differences and so doesn't subscribe to any one path.

Based upon early experiences he developed the opinion there was more to us than surgeons can remove and that just because an experience wasn't commonly shared by everyone did not mean it was necessarily 'fantasy'.

Eventually he found he wasn't alone. Many people had experienced the same things he had. They just didn't tend to talk about them in general conversation. This has led him on a lifelong pursuit to better understand the mystical elements of the multi-verse and our connection to them.